For the full collection visit

charitablebookings.com/**recipe-books**

CHARITABLE **BOOKINGS**

SIGNATURE♥DISH

UK

To:

From:

Message:

3 STEPS TO UNLOCK YOUR 250 U.K. RECIPES

1 Download the free **CHARITABLE BOOKINGS** lifestyle app.

2 Go to 📖 *Recipes*, tap on **001-250**, then tap on **Unlock**.

3 Enter the **unique code** to unlock these 250 **CHARITABLE BOOKINGS** Signature Dish U.K. main course recipes and, in addition, a donation will be made by **CHARITABLE BOOKINGS** to a charity of your choice at absolutely no cost to you.

SCRATCH OFF TO REVEAL

Foreword

It is my pleasure to write the foreword to this wonderful recipe book collection that showcases 1,500 of the best loved chefs working at the finest restaurants, private members clubs and 5* hotels throughout the U.K. and America, while knowing that together we are all helping to support countless deserving causes.

In an increasingly cashless society we set up the lifestyle restaurant and hotel reservations platform, CHARITABLE **BOOKINGS**, as a simple way to help charities generate additional unrestricted funds and awareness at no cost to themselves, while continuing our ethos of encouraging individuals and organisations to support good causes as part of their daily life.

Individuals can choose from thousands of U.K. and U.S. registered charities who are supported by CHARITABLE **BOOKINGS** every time they eat out or book a hotel. This costs the individual and the charity nothing and we hope that this will become an essential free tool to help charities boost their bottom line and to enable corporate organisations to increase the funds they generate for good causes. Of course, we are indebted to the support from our many thousands of restaurant and hotel partners who will help make a real difference to the lives of those in need both now and in the future.

With so many excellent restaurants and hotels on board we decided to showcase some of the chefs in what was planned as a small section on our app and website. The response from chefs and restaurants was so overwhelming that we made the decision to publish our first CHARITABLE **BOOKINGS** recipe book. We have now gone on to create a collection of books, each unlocking 250 recipes on the lifestyle app.

We hope you will enjoy these delightful books in the knowledge that every copy has generated funds for good causes.

Having encouraged you to cook at home with these books and via the app, we would now like to encourage you to go out and eat. Use CHARITABLE **BOOKINGS** for your personal and business restaurant bookings and help us support the restaurant industry and the causes dear to your heart, making a positive difference to those less fortunate.

It's very easy to use and you can select a different charity to benefit every time you go out – with it costing you absolutely nothing to do so!

I hope you enjoy the book collection and download all the recipes. Thank you again for supporting those wonderful organisations that do so much good for so many.

Lord Fink

Editor's welcome

Welcome to the CHARITABLE **BOOKINGS** Signature Dish recipe book collection, an initiative of CHARITABLE **BOOKINGS** that aims to support up to 500,000 U.K. & U.S. registered causes.

Firstly, I would like to take this opportunity to dedicate these books to my late father, Michael, who continues to inspire and motivate me and taught me to appreciate great ingredients, the importance of tunnel vision and to always try to do good by others.

With this in mind I decided I wanted to do something different, something big, that hadn't been attempted before. I wanted to bring together a wide variety of the best loved chefs from the world's leading restaurants, private members clubs and 5* hotels, in support of thousands of charities, while creating the perfect gift for all foodies. The huge number of recipes available within this collection shows you really can't judge a book by its cover!

Compiling this collection to date has been a massive undertaking, but it has been an enjoyable journey, allowing me to bring together a selection of 1,500 mouth-watering main course signature dish recipes through the collection for you to enjoy at home. From simple hearty meals and exotic spicy creations, to Michelin star wonders and dinner party crowd pleasers, we have assembled a fantastic array of delicious restaurant quality recipes to give everyone the opportunity to cook like a professional chef.

What makes these cook books different is that not only can you be inspired by the wonderful array of recipes, but by simply downloading the free CHARITABLE **BOOKINGS** lifestyle app and entering the unique code found at the front of each book, you will unlock 250 recipes for you to access from your iOS, Android smart phones or tablet.

This ever growing book collection is a perfect complement to the CHARITABLE **BOOKINGS** lifestyle, restaurant and hotel booking platform. Allowing you to not only enjoy fantastic benefits, but also to raise unrestricted funds for a charity of your choice every time you make either a hotel booking or restaurant reservation via the app or charitable**bookings**.com, at absolutely no cost to you.

Each chef's dish will not only brighten up your table, but will help brighten up the lives of people who need help and support. By entering the unique code found at front of this book, a donation will be made by CHARITABLE **BOOKINGS** to a charity of your choice at absolutely no cost to you. A delicious way to support good causes.

We hope you'll find some exciting recipes here to try and with any luck you will buy these books as a gift for your family members, friends and colleagues, so all the foodies you know can enjoy these delicious inspiring recipes and this ever growing worldwide philanthropic collaboration.

David Johnstone
Editor-In-Chief

500 LEADING CHEFS' SIGNATURE DISH RECIPES FROM THE FOUR CORNERS OF THE UNITED KINGDOM...

Each of the two U.K. volumes of the CHARITABLE **BOOKINGS** Signature Dish recipe book collection unlocks **250** mouth-watering dishes from **250** of the leading chefs from the finest restaurants, private members' clubs and 5* hotels throughout the four corners of the United Kingdom.

Each book contains 50 recipes and a **unique code** that unlocks all **250** on the free CHARITABLE **BOOKINGS** lifestyle app. On entering the **unique code** you will also have the opportunity to select a cause close to your heart, from a growing list of over 500,000 U.K. & U.S. registered charities, CHARITABLE **BOOKINGS** will make a donation to that cause at absolutely no cost to you.

charitablebookings.com/**recipe-books**

CHARITABLE **BOOKINGS**

SIGNATURE♡DISH

UK

1,000 LEADING CHEFS' SIGNATURE DISH RECIPES FROM ACROSS ALL 50 STATES OF AMERICA...

Each of the four U.S. volumes of the CHARITABLE **BOOKINGS** Signature Dish recipe book collection unlocks **250** mouth-watering dishes from **250** of the leading chefs from the finest restaurants and 5* hotels from across all 50 states of America.

Each book contains 50 recipes and a **unique code** that unlocks all **250** on the free CHARITABLE **BOOKINGS** lifestyle app. On entering the **unique code** you will also have the opportunity to select a cause close to your heart, from a growing list of over 500,000 U.K. & U.S. registered charities, CHARITABLE **BOOKINGS** will make a donation to that cause at absolutely no cost to you.

charitable**bookings**.com/**recipe-books**

CHARITABLE **BOOKINGS**

SIGNATURE♡DISH

USA

L♥VE...

CHARITABLE **BOOKINGS** is the FREE lifestyle app that has fantastic benefits and also gives back to your favourite charity at absolutely no cost to you.

CHARITABLE
BOOKINGS

charitable**bookings**.com

Download on the
App Store

GET IT ON
Google Play

Book at over 8,500 restaurants across the U.K. and £1/$1 will be donated for EVERY diner, by CHARITABLE BOOKINGS, to a charity of your choice at absolutely no cost to you.

"ingenious"
Sunday Times Magazine

"ethical eating"
Daily Mail

L♥VE...

Book at over 250,000 hotels across the world and CHARITABLE BOOKINGS will donate £1/$1 per guest for EVERY night's stay to a charity of your choice at absolutely no cost to you.

"Unlike any other online UK booking platform"

Institute of Fundraising

Enjoy access to 1,000s of Secret Tips including the best restaurant table numbers to ask for when making a booking.

"Everyone is able to support charitable fundraising while dining out at absolutely no cost to themselves. Charity just got so much easier"

Style

L♥VE...

DEALS?

Enjoy Deals at selected restaurants including a complimentary round of drinks for you and all your friends.

"This could be the most enjoyable and easiest way to do good"
ELLE Decoration

Enjoy collecting Loyalty Points on selected restaurant and hotel bookings and redeeming them for gifts and rewards or donate them to a charity of your choice.

"Good deeds you can do.. No 1"
Evening Standard

LOVE...

Enjoy reading free articles on the go from the worlds of luxury and philanthropy.

"Pick of the best"
Exclusively British

Enjoy free recipes EVERY week from the CHARITABLE BOOKINGS Signature Dish cookbook collection, created by 1,500 of the best loved chefs from the U.K.'s & U.S.'s leading restaurants, private members clubs and 5* hotels.

"Very, very special"
COUNTRY LIFE

"Website of the week"
The SUN

Enjoy playing Swipe daily for free for the chance to WIN money for your favourite charity and individual prizes worth up to £7,500/$10,000 at the world's most luxurious brands including: Harrods, Agent Provocateur, Louboutin, Gucci, Dunhill, Prada, Cartier and many more.

Enjoy Giving Back for FREE to a cause close to your heart from a growing list of over 500,000 U.K. and U.S. registered charities by using the CHARITABLE BOOKINGS lifestyle app today.

"A way in which to help thousands of people less fortunate, through a simple everyday thing"

Made in Shoreditch

250 CHEFS

and a selection of

50 RECIPES

Browse the following pages to preview a selection of 50 Signature Dish recipes ready for you to try.

Use the **unique code** at the beginning of this book to unlock the **250** Signature Dish main course recipes on the free CHARITABLE **BOOKINGS** lifestyle app.

	Tom Aikens	*Tom's Kitchen*	7 hour-braised shoulder of lamb with onions, thyme and balsamic
	Paul Ainsworth	*Paul Ainsworth at Number 6*	Crispy Porthilly oysters
	David Alexander	*Glenapp Castle*	Beetroot risotto with feta, parmesan and aged balsamic
	Paul Askew	*The Art School Restaurant*	Peterhead halibut fillet with saffon potato risotto, steamed oyster and charred leeks
	Craig Atchinson	*Grand Hotel and Spa York*	North atlantic stone bass with fennel, langoustines, coastal herbs and bisque
	Frances Atkins	*Yorke Arms*	Lacquered English veal with lobster, strawberry and cabbage cake
	Pascal Aussignac	*Club Gascon*	Roast scallops with polenta and squid ink sauce
	Dario Avenca	*Morton's*	Poached wild turbot, with lardo di colonnata and fish red wine sauce
	Harvey Ayliffe	*34 Mayfair*	34 Mayfair's lobster mac
	Richard Bainbridge	*Benedicts*	Pot roast chicken with fondant potatoes and watercress

Foodie fact #1
Lemons contain more sugar
than strawberries.

Mark Greenaway - *Restaurant Mark Greenaway*
Roasted wild salmon and cucumber
Unlock these 250 recipes on the free CHARITABLE **BOOKINGS** lifestyle app.

TOM AIKENS
Tom's Kitchen

7 HOUR-BRAISED SHOULDER OF LAMB with onions, thyme and balsamic

SERVES 4 | PREPARATION TIME 30 MINUTES | COOKING TIME 7-8 HOURS

For the Braised Shoulder of Lamb
2.5kg (*5.5lbs*) lamb shoulder
150ml (*5fl oz*) olive oil
20g (*0.7oz*) fresh thyme, chopped
2 bulbs of garlic, cloves peeled
sea salt and black pepper
8 medium onions, peeled
350ml (*12fl oz*) balsamic vinegar

For the Mashed Potato
600g (*21oz*) peeled potatoes, quartered
12g (*0.4oz*) salt
200g (*7oz*) butter
150ml (*5fl oz*) milk, warmed
1 pinch of black pepper

To cook the lamb, place a large casserole pot onto a medium gas and add the oil. Season and place the shoulder into the pot once the oil is hot. Colour for 3-4 minutes on each side until nicely caramelised. Remove the lamb and put to one side. Colour the onions for 4-5 minutes, stirring now and again. After suitably cooked, add the garlic and thyme and place the lamb back on top.

Place the casserole dish into the oven at 110°C (*230°F*) and cover with a lid. Leave to cook for 2-2.5 hours, remove the onions once they are soft. Carry on cooking the lamb for another 2.5-3 hours. Add the vinegar and carry on cooking without the lid so the vinegar reduces as the lamb cooks, basting the lamb every 30 minutes, being careful not to reduce it too much.

When the lamb is nice and tender, add the onions and garlic back and reduce the vinegar to a nice, thick consistency.

To make the mashed potato, place the potatoes into a pan of cold water with 10g (*0.3oz*) salt and bring to boil. Turn the heat down and simmer for 30 minutes, then tip the potatoes into a colander to drain well. Place the cooked potatoes back into the pan and remove the moisture on a low heat for 1 minute, then add the butter, remaining salt, pepper and warm milk slowly while you mash.

To serve, slice or shred the meat from the bone and place the casserole dish in the centre of the table. Enjoy.

PAUL AINSWORTH
Paul Ainsworth at Number 6

CRISPY PORTHILLY OYSTERS
SERVES 4 | PREPARATION TIME 30 MINUTES | COOKING TIME 10 MINUTES

For the Oysters
12 large oysters
2 egg whites, let down with a
splash of water
200g (7oz) panko breadcrumbs
12 fine slices salami Milano

For the Apple and Fennel Salad
2 medium heads fennel
2 Granny Smith apples
fresh lime juice
4 stems bright green chervil

To Serve
sea shells and hay
pebbles
1 pinch of rock salt

To prepare the oysters, shuck and gently wash in cold water. Pass the oyster juices through a fine sieve to remove any grit. Pop the oysters into a container, cover with cling film and keep in the fridge until required. Scrub the shells clean and sterilise them in boiling water, ready to use later for serving.

To make the apple and fennel salad, trim the fennel tops off and peel the layers apart. Discarding the outer layer, trim off any chunky areas and slice into large, neat rectangles. Next, finely chop to 3mm slices and coat with a tablespoon of lime juice. Chop the apple in fine slices so it matches the fennel. Combine together with the fennel, ensuring the salad is well coated with fresh lime juice so it cannot discolour. Finely chop the chervil leaves and add a large pinch to the salad. Taste and add more lime juice if desired. Dip the oysters in the egg white, then the panko breadcrumbs. Deep fry at 190°C (375°F) until golden and crisp, taking care not to overcook them. The oyster should be just cooked in the centre.

To serve, decorate 4 plates with pebbles and hay. Divide the oyster shells onto the plates and fill each shell with the apple and fennel salad. Place the oysters, plump side up, on top of the salad, then sprinkle with a little rock sea salt. To finish, drape a slice of salami over each oyster at the last second and serve immediately.

Ed Baines	*Randall and Aubin*	Crispy duck salad
Andrew Baird	*Longueville Manor Hotel*	Halibut steak with new season peas à la française
John Barber and Nicolas Rafa	*Bar Boulud*	Pithivier de pigeon and foie gras with preserved lemon and mushrooms
Matt Barker	*The Westwood*	Westwood's bone-in ribeye steak marinated in molasses, bourbon and thyme with Café de Paris grill butter
George Barson	*Kitty Fisher's*	Lamb breast and loin with wild garlic and smoked anchovy
Alessandro Bay	*Diciannove Italian Restaurant and Wine*	Beef and pork ragout tagliatelle
Marcus Bean	*The Brompton Cookery School*	Chicken supremes in lovage butter en papillote
Matthew Beardshall	*Wild Garlic*	Rump of Cotswold lamb with marinated aubergine and persillade
Herbert Berger	*Herbert Berger at Innholders*	Poached fillet of new season lamb with spring vegetables and mint broth
Daniel Birk	*Social Eating House*	Lamb neck fillets

Foodie fact #2
Cucumbers are 96% water.

Philip Corrick - *Royal Automobile Club at Woodcote Park Clubhouse*
Rosettes of venison with blueberries and spiced pear
Unlock these 250 recipes on the free CHARITABLE **BOOKINGS** lifestyle app.

PASCAL AUSSIGNAC
Club Gascon

ROAST SCALLOPS with polenta and squid ink sauce
SERVES 4 | PREPARATION TIME 30 MINUTES | COOKING TIME 1 HOUR

Equipment
siphon with N2O
For the Roast Scallops
8 large scallops in shell
50ml (1.8fl oz) olive oil
salt and pepper
250ml (9fl oz) water
1g (0.03oz) espelette pepper
25g (1oz) butter

For the Polenta
30g (1.1oz) squid ink
50g (1.7oz) instant polenta
500ml (16fl oz) milk
4 cloves of garlic, crushed
50ml (1.8fl oz) olive oil
2g (0.07oz) espelette pepper

To Serve
1 handful of rocket leaves per
serving
8 sterilised scallop shells, boil in
water for 5 minutes

Shuck the scallops from their shells, save the orange roes. Pull off the little nuggets of muscle from the sides. Wash the scallops well, pat dry and store in the fridge.

To make the sauce, heat half the olive oil in a small pan and sauté the scallop roes and muscle nuggets with a little salt and pepper, for 3-5 minutes. Cover with 250ml (8.8fl oz) of water and simmer for about 10 minutes. Strain the liquid into a small bowl, pressing down with the back of a spoon to extract all the juices, and discard the trimmings. Add the remaining olive oil and the espelette pepper, and whisk together. At this stage, if you don't have a siphon to make the foam, spoon the squid ink into the strained liquid.

To cook the scallops, heat the butter in a small non-stick frying pan and fry the scallops for about a minute on each side, seasoning in the pan.

To make the squid ink polenta foam, begin by heating the milk in a large non-stick saucepan and add the garlic. Add the olive oil and espelette pepper. Then, when the milk is just on the boil, turn the heat to medium, pour in the polenta and squeeze in the squid ink in a steady stream, stirring briskly with a long-handled wooden spoon. The mixture will thicken and begin to plop and splutter, which is normal. Partly cover the pan and turn the heat to low. Cook for 10 minutes. Remove and let it stand.

To serve, place the squid ink polenta into the siphon and eject carefully into the bottom of the sterilised shells. Top with the scallops and the sauce. Garnish with a handful of rocket and serve hot.

RICHARD BAINBRIDGE

Benedicts

POT ROAST CHICKEN with fondant potatoes and watercress

SERVES 4 | PREPARATION TIME 15 MINUTES + OVERNIGHT SOAKING | COOKING TIME 90 MINUTES

For the Pot Roasted Chicken
1 chicken crown
1 carrot, chopped
1 shallot, chopped
2 celery sticks, chopped
50ml (*1.8fl oz*) white wine
10g (*0.35oz*) garden herbs
1 tbsp rapeseed oil

For the Fondant Potatoes
12 red potatoes, cut into cylinders
150g (*5.3oz*) salted butter
water, to cover
1 sprig of thyme
2 cloves of garlic
salt

For the Watercress Purée
1 egg yolk
150g (*5.3oz*) watercress
25ml (*1fl oz*) cider vinegar
100ml (*3.5fl oz*) rapeseed oil
20g ice cubes

For the chicken, start by preheating an oven to 200°C (*390°F*). Place the vegetables, wine and herbs into a clay pot that has been soaked in water overnight. Season the chicken crown and colour in a large frying pan with the rapeseed oil. Place on top of the vegetables, close the lid and leave in the oven for 40 minutes. Remove the lid and bake for another 15 minutes. Take the pot out of the oven, cover with a tea towel and allow to rest for 15 minutes.

To make the fondant potatoes, place all the ingredients into a pot on a high heat and bring to the boil. Once boiling, turn the heat down to a rolling boil and take care to keep the potatoes from sticking. By the time they're cooked, all that should remain are the potato cylinders and a butter coating. Once coloured, leave in the butter until ready to serve.

For the watercress purée, blitz the egg yolk, watercress and vinegar into a smooth purée. Put in the ice cubes and slowly add the oil, continuing to blend on a medium speed. Once all the oil is in, a bright green watercress purée should remain. Season to taste and place in the fridge.

To serve, assemble the dish as pictured and top with an optional watercress salad, lemon juice, salt, pepper and a little rapeseed oil.

	Galton Blackiston	*Morston Hall*	Crab toasties with potato-wrapped quails' eggs
	Raymond Blanc	*Brasserie Blanc*	Roast pheasant and winter vegetables
	Jeremy Bloor	*OXO Tower Restaurant, Bar and Brasserie*	Truffle burrata with asparagus, puntarelle, basil seeds, pea gel and lemon oil
	Heston Blumenthal	*The Fat Duck*	Triple cooked chips and steak
	Tommy Boland	*Bird of Smithfield*	Pan roasted fillet of wild cornish turbot with truffled linguine and braised chicken wing
	Stéphane Borie	*The Checkers*	Crab and sweet potato cannelloni with coconut coulis and kaffir lime dressing
	Claude Bosi	*Bibendum*	Cornish cod à la Grenobloise
	Michael Bremner	*64 Degrees*	Black bream ceviche
	Henry Brosi	*The Dorchester*	White onion risotto with white chocolate, scallops and white truffle
	Michael Brown	*Daphne's*	Chicken alla Milanese with gremolata

Foodie fact #3
An ostrich egg needs to be
boiled for over an hour to get
a hard boiled egg.

Daniel Galmiche - *The Gore Hotel*
Pan-roasted wild halibut with tomato confit, feta, rosemary crisps and aioli
Unlock these 250 recipes on the free CHARITABLE **BOOKINGS** lifestyle app.

ED BAINES
Randall and Aubin

CRISPY DUCK SALAD

SERVES 4 | PREPARATION TIME 20 MINUTES | COOKING TIME 45 MINUTES

For the Dish
2 duck legs
3 star anise
½ head of garlic
1 thumb of ginger, roughly chopped
20g (0.7oz) coriander stalks, roughly chopped
1 tsp Chinese five-spice powder
lime wedges, to serve

For the Duck Sauce
4 tbsp tomato ketchup
½ orange, juiced
1 tbsp each honey, soy sauce and sesame oil

For the Salad
1 packet of egg noodles
4 bunches of watercress, stalks removed
110g (3.9oz) white radish, peeled and ribboned
50g (1.8oz) bean shoots
1 bunch of spring onions, trimmed
20g (0.7oz) coriander leaves
1 tbsp sesame seeds, lightly toasted
dry shrimps, optional
Asian sprouts or cresses, optional

For the Soy and Sesame Dressing
1 tsp soy sauce
1 tsp rice vinegar
1 clove of garlic, peeled and crushed
1 small piece of ginger, grated
1 tbsp sesame oil
3 tbsp vegetable or corn oil

Cover the duck with the water, add the herbs and spices and simmer gently for 45 minutes. Remove the duck from the stock and set it aside to cool. Skim the fat off the stock and use it as a base to make an Asian soup.

To make the duck sauce, whisk together all the ingredients in a bowl.

To make the soy and sesame dressing, whisk all of the ingredients together.

Remove the duck meat from the bone, then cut into 1cm thick slices. Toss the duck pieces in the sauce and grill for 2 minutes until hot.

To assemble the dish, arrange the watercress on the plates, take a good handful of salad ingredients per portion and a handful of noodles in a mixing bowl and drizzle with dressing. Place over the plated watercress, top with warm duck, sprinkle with sesame seeds, coriander leaves and finish with a wedge of lime.

ANDREW BAIRD
Longueville Manor Hotel

HALIBUT STEAK with new season peas à la Francaise
SERVES 4 | PREPARATION TIME 15 MINUTES | COOKING TIME 10 MINUTES

For the Dish
4 x 180g (6.3oz) halibut steaks, or cod
10ml (0.35fl oz) pomace oil
1 knob of Jersey butter
60ml (2.1fl oz) fish stock
For the Peas
550g (19.4oz) butter
10g (0.35oz) flour

40g (1.4oz) pancetta, cubed
200ml (7fl oz) chicken stock or cube
20g (0.7oz) carrot, diced
20g (0.7oz) potato, diced
60g (2.1oz) baby silverskin onions, peeled
300g (11oz) new season peas, shelled, frozen peas can be

substituted
20g (0.7oz) broad beans, peeled
To Serve
1 little gem lettuce
salt and freshly ground black pepper

Preheat the oven to 180°C (355°F).

To make the peas, mix 10g (0.35oz) the butter with the flour to make a beurre meunière, a thickening agent. Put the remaining butter in a saucepan and heat. Add the pancetta and cook until it changes colour. Add the chicken stock and bring to a simmer, then add the carrots, potato and silverskin onions and cook until tender. Add the peas and broad beans. Bring back to a simmer. At this point break the beurre meunière into small pieces and gently whisk into the pea mixture. This will slightly thicken the stock and give it more body. Keep warm.

To cook the halibut, simply heat an ovenproof frying pan. Add a little pomace oil and when it starts to lightly smoke add the fish. Cook until golden brown on one side. Turn the fish over, add a knob of butter and the fish stock. Place in the oven for approximately 8 minutes.

To serve, at the last minute halve the little gem lengthways and shred. Add to the peas and beans. As soon as the lettuce has wilted, place in a bowl plate, remove the fish from the oven and place on top.

	Russell Brown	*Sienna*	Butternut squash and old Winchester agnolotti with sage butter
	Sean Burbidge	*The Ivy Market Grill*	Roasted butternut squash with buckwheat grains, chickpeas, pomegranate and feta, harissa yoghurt and coriander dressing
	Chris Burt	*The Peach Tree*	Clams and ham
	Shawn Butcher	*Langan's Brasserie*	Slow roast Dingley Dell pork belly with a honey, chilli and ginger glaze
	Adam Byatt	*Trinity Restaurant*	Roast grouse with white polenta, cobnuts and blackberry
	Graham Campbell	*Castlehill*	Highland venison with pear, chicory and chocolate
	Claudio Cardoso	*Sushi Samba*	Samba salad
	Phil Carmichael	*Berners Tavern*	Roasted Cornish cod with fregola, tomato and samphire salad, tomato water, crispy squid
	Brad Carter	*Carters of Moseley*	Partridge with creamed polenta and Wiltshire truffle
	Rhys Cattermoul	*Nobu Berkeley St*	Chilean sea bass with truffle miso

Foodie fact #4
Neither strawberries, blackberries nor raspberries are actual berries.

Adam Byatt - *Trinity Restaurant*
Roast grouse with white polenta, cobnuts and blackberry
Unlock these 250 recipes on the free CHARITABLE **BOOKINGS** lifestyle app.

ALESSANDRO BAY

Diciannove Italian Restaurant and Wine

BEEF AND PORK RAGOUT TAGLIATELLE

SERVES 10 | PREPARATION TIME 15 MINUTES | COOKING TIME 3 HOURS 30 MINUTES

For the Dish
1kg (*2.2lb*) beef mince
1kg (*2.2lb*) pork mince
300g (*11oz*) mixed cured meat
drizzle of olive oil
1 stick of celery, finely chopped
2 carrots, finely chopped

1 large white onion, finely chopped
red wine, to cover
2 tbsp tomato purée
1 tin tomato sauce
1 bouquet garni - rosemary, thyme, bay leaves

To Serve
tagliatelle

To prepare the ragu, heat the olive oil in a large pan, add all the finely chopped vegetables and cook on a very low heat in order to sweat them. In another large sauté pan, heat the olive oil and start to cook the minced meat in small batches until golden brown, in order to eliminate all the water. Once the meat is ready, add to the vegetables until all the meat is done. Add the red wine to cover and let it evaporate completely. Once the wine is completely gone, add the tomato paste, and let it cook for a few minutes. Add the tomato sauce and some water, bring to the boil and once the sauce has reached boiling point, immediately turn down the heat to a very gentle simmer. Add a bouquet garni and let it cook for at least 2—3 hours making sure it doesn't stick to the bottom. After that time the ragu is ready.

Serve on fresh tagliatelle.

MATTHEW BEARDSHALL
Wild Garlic

RUMP OF COTSWOLD LAMB with marinated aubergine and persillade

SERVES 4 | PREPARATION TIME 20 MINUTES (PLUS OVERNIGHT TO MARINATE) | COOKING TIME 40 MINUTES

For the Lamb
4 x 250g (8.8oz) lamb rumps
vegetable oil for frying

For the Persillade
½ bunch curly parsley
½ bunch wild garlic leaf
½ lemon, zested
1 shallot, finely diced
2 cloves of garlic, finely chopped

For the Marinated Aubergine
15g (0.53oz) ginger, roughly chopped
3 cloves of garlic, roughly chopped
1 red chilli, roughly chopped
3 vine tomatoes, roughly chopped
60g (2.1oz) honey
60ml (2.1fl oz) red wine vinegar

1 sprig of rosemary
1 fresh bay leaf
1 sprig of thyme
1 aubergine
40ml (1.4fl oz) extra virgin rapeseed oil, for frying

To Serve
purple sprouting broccoli
cavolo nero
kale
green beans

To make the marinated aubergine, place the ginger, garlic, chilli, tomatoes, honey, vinegar and herbs in a pan and bring to the boil, then pour into a deep metal dish. Cut the aubergine into wedges and colour the cut sides in a smoking hot pan with a good splash of oil. Transfer the charred aubergine into the warm marinade. Leave to cool and refrigerate overnight in a sealed container. This is best marinated overnight but can be used straight away.

To make the persillade, chop the parsley and wild garlic roughly, taking care not to bruise it; a sharp knife is a must. Simply mix all the ingredients together. It will keep for a few days in the fridge, but is best made and eaten fresh. Try mixing any leftovers with oil and utilise as a pesto.

To make the lamb rump, preheat the oven to 200°C (390°F). Seal the lamb rump in a hot pan with a touch of oil and colour all sides until golden brown. Transfer to the oven for 8 minutes, then leave to rest for a further 8 minutes.

To assemble the dish, roll each lamb rump in some of the persillade, then slice into 3. Gently warm the aubergine in the marinade over a low heat. Arrange on the plate as pictured. Finish with a spoonful of persillade and garnish with the chopped chilli, garlic and tomato from the marinade. Serve with seasonal vegetables.

	Tom Cenci	*Duck & Waffle*	Miso glazed rabbit with cauliflower purée and pie crust
	Sandia Chang	*Bubbledogs*	Buffalo hot dog with horny devils
	Nik Chappell	*The Slaughters Manor House*	Soy poached turbot with girolles and mushroom dashi
	Karl Cheetham	*Gliffaes*	Scallops with crisp chicken wing and pea cream
	Ian Clark	*Gallimaufry*	Hake with curried cauliflower, almond and kohlrabi bhaji
	Derry Clarke	*L'Ecrivain*	Crispy duck breast with sage and thyme glazed butternut squash, shallots, cured bacon and star anise jus
	Sally Clarke	*Clarke's*	Sea bass baked with potato and fennel
	Daniel Clifford	*Midsummer House*	Venison with chervil, elderberry and cavolo nero
	Claude Compton	*Claude's Kitchen*	Line-caught cod with cabbage, lovage, buttermilk and new potatoes
	Gennaro Contaldo	*Celebrity Chef*	La Genovese con pennette slow-cooked onion and veal sauce with pasta

Foodie fact #5
A bunch of bananas is actually called a hand.

Tom Kerridge - *The Hand and Flowers*
Rump steak stew
Unlock these 250 recipes on the free CHARITABLE **BOOKINGS** lifestyle app.

RAYMOND BLANC

Brasserie Blanc

ROAST PHEASANT AND WINTER VEGETABLES

SERVES 4 | PREPARATION TIME 20 MINUTES | COOKING TIME 1 HOUR

For the Roast Pheasant
2 x 800g (28oz) hen pheasants
50g (1.8oz) butter
50ml (1.8fl oz) vegetable oil
2 tsp game seasoning
100ml (3.5fl oz) red wine
100ml (3.5fl oz) port
2 sprigs of thyme

For the Game Seasoning
100g (3.5oz) coarse sea salt
½ tbsp coarse ground black
peppercorns
1 tsp juniper berries
2 star anise
5g stick of cinnamon
2 dried bay leafs
5g (0.2oz) garlic, freshly peeled

To Serve
roasted winter vegetables

To make the game seasoning, blend all the ingredients in a food processor for around 2 minutes. Transfer the blended mixture to a sterilised container with a lid, and allow to rest and infuse while preparing the pheasant.

To make the roast pheasants, begin by preheating an oven to 190°C (375°F). In a heavy-bottomed frying pan over a low heat, very gently brown the birds all over in foaming butter and oil, for approximately 5 minutes or until golden brown. Sprinkle the birds with game seasoning and place them in a roasting tin. Transfer to the oven and cook for 30 minutes, routinely checking and turning halfway through. Once cooked, cover and set aside in a warm place to rest. Meanwhile, strain the excess fat from the roasting tin and add the wine, port and fresh thyme. Reduce over a high heat, until you have two thirds of the original volume, making sure to scrape the flavour from the bottom of the pan. Season to taste if necessary and strain into a warmed jug.

To serve, carve the meat from the birds, pour over the jus and plate with roasted winter vegetables.

CLAUDE BOSI
Bibendum

CORNISH COD A LA GRENOBLOISE
SERVES 4 | PREPARATION TIME 15 MINUTES | COOKING TIME 30 MINUTES

Equipment
steamer
For the Dish
500g (*18oz*) ratte potatoes,
crushed
100g (*3.5oz*) butter, to be
browned for beurre noisette

1 tsp capers
1 tsp croutons
lemon zest, to garnish
1 dash of sherry vinegar
4 x 100g (*3.5oz*) fillets of cod
salt, to season

For the Grenobloise Sauce
250g (*8.8oz*) butter
½ lemon, juiced
750g (*26.4fl oz*) milk
150g (*5.3oz*) bread trims
salt, to taste

First make the beurre noisette by browning the butter in a pan, whisking occasionally until the butter resembles a nut brown colour. Add the lemon juice and leave to cool slightly. Toast off your bread trim and gently warm the milk. Add the trims and infuse for 5 minutes. Pass through a sieve and add to the brown butter. Season and foam the sauce with a hand blender.

Cook the potatoes in salted water. Peel and lightly crush with a fork. Season with salt and sherry vinegar. Add the capers and croutons on top.

To finish, season the fish and steam. Place the potatoes in the centre of the plate, spoon the fish on top and sprinkle with the lemon zest and lemon segments. Pour over the foamed butter sauce and serve.

	Shay Cooper	*The Goring Hotel*	Plaice fillet with gem lettuce, cucumber and potted shrimp butter
	Philip Corrick	*The Royal Automobile Club at Woodcote Park*	Rosettes of venison with blueberries and spiced pear
	Richard Corrigan	*Bentley's Oyster Bar & Grill*	Royal fish pie
	David Coulson	*Peace and Loaf*	Halibut and chicken pie
	Jim Cowie	*Captain's Galley Seafood Restaurant*	Mussels steamed with lemongrass, basil chilli and coconut juice
	Alan Coxon	*Celebrity Chef*	Autumnal chicken tagine with a casserole of pumpkin, chestnuts, apples and prunes
	Alex Craciun	*Sosharu*	Tonkatsu crumbed pork with radish salad
	Stephen Crane	*Ockenden Manor*	Pigeon with boudin blanc, croquette, red cabbage ketchup, white asparagus, flower sprouts and caramelised apple
	Fabio Cuofano	*Goat*	Sea bass with miso glaze, baby spinach, fennel and pomodori secchi
	Ollie Dabbous	*Celebrity Chef*	Coddled egg with smoked butter and mushrooms

Foodie fact #6
There are close to 10,000 varieties of apples.

Tom Kitchin - *The Kitchin*
Shellfish rockpool
Unlock these 250 recipes on the free CHARITABLE **BOOKINGS** lifestyle app.

MICHAEL BREMNER

64 Degrees

BLACK BREAM CEVICHE
SERVES 5 | PREPARATION TIME 15 MINUTES

For the Ceviche
250g (*8.8oz*) fresh black bream fillets
1 stick celery, keep celery leaves for garnish

½ red chilli
½cm piece of ginger
100ml (*3.5fl oz*) water
1 lime, juiced
salt to taste

For the Garnish
celery, diced
red chilli, diced
celery leaves

Make a very fine dice with a small amount of the celery and chilli and set aside to use as garnish for the ceviche.

To make the ceviche, blitz the remaining celery, chilli and ginger with the water before passing through a fine sieve, then add the lime juice. Dice the bream into 1cm pieces and add to the ceviche mix. Season to taste with a little salt.

To serve, portion into 5 bowls. Garnish with the finely diced celery and chilli, as well as the celery leaves.

HENRY BROSI
The Dorchester

WHITE ONION RISOTTO with white chocolate, scallops and white truffle
SERVES 4 | PREPARATION TIME 5 MINUTES | COOKING TIME 30 MINUTES

For the Scallops
8 scallops, cleaned and trimmed
sea salt and pepper
1 drizzle of olive oil
1 splash of lemon juice
For the Onion Confit
2 large onions
goose fat
salt and pepper

For the Risotto
150g (5.3oz) Arborio risotto rice
extra virgin olive oil
100ml (3.5fl oz) white wine
1l (35fl oz) chicken stock
sea salt and white pepper
10g (0.35oz) white truffle
2 tablespoons mascarpone
100g (3.5oz) Parmesan

1 lemon, juiced
50g (1.8oz) white chocolate
25g (0.9oz) butter
To Serve
10g (0.35oz) white truffle

To prepare the onion confit, cook very thinly sliced onions with goose fat over a very low heat until the onions are soft. Season and strain the onions. Keep aside for further use.

To prepare the risotto, heat up a pan and add some of the olive oil. Fry the rice quickly without colouring and cook for a further one minute. Add the white wine to the rice and cook whilst stirring continuously. Cook until the liquid is absorbed. Add the stock 100ml (3.5fl oz) at a time and keep stirring until the rice has cooked and is slightly al dente. Season to taste. Add half of the sliced truffle and then add the mascarpone cheese, Parmesan cheese, white onions, juice from the lemon and finally the white chocolate and melted butter.

To prepare the scallops, season then heat a non-stick frying pan and add a little olive oil. Fry the scallops until golden brown. Turn over and cook for a further minute. Add a splash of lemon juice and then take the scallops out of the pan. Cut the scallops in half.

To serve, spoon the risotto onto the plates and place the scallops on top. Shave the remaining truffle and scatter over the top.

	Berwyn Davies	*The Glasshouse*	Venison with salsify purée with roasted salsify and pine gnocchi
	Scott Davies	*The Three Chimneys*	Loin of Highland venison in onion ash with charred beetroot, salt-baked celeriac and reindeer moss
	Anthony Demetre	*Wild Honey*	Saddle of rabbit with shoulder and leg cottage pie
	Phil Dixon	*Mulberry Restaurant at Langshott Manor*	Roasted quail with lavender and smoke
	Mark Dodson	*The Masons Arms*	Loin of venison with poached pear and blue cheese gratin
	Steven Doherty	*The First Floor Cafe*	Cullen skink
	Javier Dominguez Santos	*Rocpool Reserve Hotel*	Hickory smoked spring chicken jambonette with sweetcorn purée, pickled girolle mushrooms and piquillo pepper dressing
	William Drabble	*Seven Park Place*	Griddled sea bass with stuffed courgettes, tomatoes, olives and basil
	Steve Drake	*Sorrel*	Jerusalem artichoke panna cotta with veal sweetbreads, Wiltshire truffle and cep biscuit
	Andrew Du Bourg	*The Elderflower*	Black sheep with caramelised cauliflower and roast root vegetables

Foodie fact #7
95% of US avocados can be traced to
one tree planted in 1926 by postman
Rudolf Hass.

Dario Avenca - *Morton's*
Poached wild turbot, with lardo di colonnata and fish red wine sauce
Unlock these 250 recipes on the free CHARITABLE **BOOKINGS** lifestyle app.

CLAUDIO CARDOSO

Sushi Samba

SAMBA SALAD

SERVES 1 | PREPARATION TIME 20 MINUTES | COOKING TIME 3 MINUTES

For the Salad
50g (*1.8oz*) kabocha squash
30g (*1.1oz*) baby spinach
20g (*0.7oz*) heritage carrot shavings
20g (*0.7oz*) green and white asparagus, ribboned
10g (*0.35oz*) heritage beet, finely sliced
10g (*0.35oz*) radish shavings

25g (*0.9oz*) red and yellow bell pepper batons
5g (*0.2oz*) enoki mushrooms
10g (*0.35oz*) caramelised macadamias
3g (*0.11oz*) mixed micro cress
1 pinch of Maldon salt
For the Truffle Honey Ponzu Sauce
1 large drizzle of soy sauce

1 large drizzle of orange juice
1 large drizzle of truffle oil
For the Samba Dressing
200g (*7oz*) mango
200g (*7oz*) red apple
50ml (*1.8fl oz*) rice vinegar
20g (*0.7oz*) onion
50g (*1.8oz*) tomato
1 pinch of salt

To make the salad, grill the kabocha for 3 minutes. Combine the soy, orange juice and truffle oil, mixing well, and marinate the squash in the mixture for 2 minutes. After this time, remove from the sauce and set to one side to rest.

Blend all the ingredients for the samba dressing together and season the spinach with it.

Take the vegetable shavings, ribbons and slices and assemble together with the grilled kabocha and enoki mushrooms. When arranging the dish, take care to place the heaviest items at the bottom and the lightest on top. Add a selection of cress and the caramelised macadamias. Sprinkle the final salad with the truffle honey ponzu and season with Maldon salt.

TOM CENCI

Duck & Waffle

MISO GLAZED RABBIT with cauliflower purée and pie crust

SERVES 2 | PREPARATION TIME 30 MINUTES | COOKING TIME 7 HOURS (CAN BE REDUCED TO 2 HOURS)

Equipment
sous vide, optional
vacuum pack bags
For the Rabbit
2 rabbit legs
100g (*3.5oz*) miso paste
100ml (*3.5fl oz*) water

For the Cauliflower Purée
1 cauliflower
50g (*1.8oz*) butter
100ml (*3.5oz*) double cream
salt and pepper
For the Cabbage
2–3 cabbage leaves
oil, for frying

For the Pie Crust
220g (*7.8oz*) plain flour
110g (*3.9oz*) suet
1 pinch of salt
12g (*0.4oz*) baking powder
170ml (*6fl oz*) water

Place the rabbit legs into a sous vide bag with the miso paste and 100ml (*3.5fl oz*) of water. Seal the bags and cook in a water bath for 7 hours at 74°C (*165°F*). If you don't have a water bath, you can braise the legs in the oven for about 2 hours but the amount of water will need to be doubled.

Slice the cauliflower into thin strips. Melt the butter in a large pan, then add the cauliflower. Gently cook until the butter foams and the cauliflower starts to brown. Pour in the double cream and blend in a food processor until smooth. Taste for seasoning.

For the pie crust, put the flour, suet, salt and baking powder into a mixing bowl. On a slow speed, gradually add the water until a dough has formed. The dough should be a bit sticky but dry enough to come away from the sides of the bowl. Roll out the dough onto a baking sheet with greaseproof paper and bake at 180°C (*355°F*) for about 15 minutes until golden brown.

To make the cabbage garnish, take a small amount of cabbage leaf and deep fry for about 30 seconds until crispy; be careful as the oil will spit from the moisture so you may need a splash guard for this.

To assemble the dish, serve the rabbit legs with the sauce it was cooked in and finish with the cauliflower purée, pieces of pie crust and crispy cabbage.

Jesse Dunford Wood	*Parlour Kensal*	Venison and ale pie, reindeer pie
Sam Dunleavy	*Eastway Brasserie*	Roast Gressingham duck with caramelised carrot purée, roast carrots and fig jus
James Durrant	*The Stafford Hotel*	Dingley Dell pork belly with caramelised onions, cockle and white bean cassoulet
Nick Edgar	*The Samling*	Pork with sage, onion and apple
Dean Edwards	*Celebrity Chef*	Chicken and chorizo lasagne
Josh Eggleton	*The Pony and Trap*	Brawn fritters with pickled red cabbage and piccalilli garnishes
David Everitt-Matthias	*Le Champignon Sauvage*	Fillet of huss with cauliflower purée and pork mince
Michael Facey	*The Laughing gravy*	Mead and malt glazed lamb shoulder with cheddar and parsnip hash browns, salt-baked turnips, glazed carrots, turnip purée and lamb jam
Phil Fanning	*Paris House*	Trout cured with chase rhubarb vodka, rhubarb gazpacho and yoghurt
Brian Fantoni	*The Westbury*	Pappardelle with wild boar ragu, herb breadcrumbs and Tuscan Pecorino

Foodie fact #8
The first mention of "sausages" is in ancient
Sumerian texts dating from over 4,000 years ago.

John Williams - *The Ritz*
Roast grouse with celeriac, salted grapes and walnuts
Unlock these 250 recipes on the free CHARITABLE **BOOKINGS** lifestyle app.

GENNARO CONTALDO

Celebrity Chef

LA GENOVESE CON PENNETTE slow-cooked onion and veal sauce with pasta

SERVES 4 | PREPARATION TIME 30 MINUTES | COOKING TIME 3 HOURS

For the Dish
800g (28oz) veal joint
2 cloves of garlic, sliced
100ml (3.5fl oz) extra virgin olive oil
2½ kg (5.5lb) large onions, sliced
1 celery stalk, finely chopped

1 large carrot, finely chopped
85g (3oz) salami, finely chopped
3 sage leaves
1 sprig of rosemary
2 bay leaves
200ml (7fl oz) dry white wine
350g (12.3oz) pennette pasta

30g (1.1oz) Pecorino Romano, grated
salt
freshly ground black pepper
To Serve
green salad

To prepare the veal, rub it all over with salt and pepper, make some incisions in the meat and poke in the garlic slices.

Heat the olive oil in a large saucepan on a medium heat. Add the veal and brown well all over. Remove from the pan and set aside. Add the onions, celery, carrot, salami and herbs. Season with salt and pepper and sweat for about 30 minutes on a low heat.

Put the meat back in the pan, add the wine and allow to evaporate. Reduce the heat to very low, cover with a lid and cook for 3 hours until the meat is very tender. Check from time to time to make sure it isn't sticking to the pan, turning the meat and stirring the onions. Remove the meat from the pan and set aside.

Using a potato masher, mash the onion mixture and season according to taste.

Cook the pennette in lightly salted, boiling water until al dente. Drain and toss with the onion mixture and any pieces of veal that have separated from the joint during cooking. Serve with grated Pecorino cheese and freshly ground black pepper.

Place the veal joint in a large dish, slice and serve as a main course with green salad.

JIM COWIE
Captain's Galley Seafood Restaurant

MUSSELS STEAMED with lemongrass, basil chilli and coconut juice
SERVES 2 | PREPARATION TIME 15 MINUTES | COOKING TIME 20 MINUTES

For the Mussels
1 can of coconut milk
1 tbsp galangal
2 stalks of lemongrass
1 fresh green chilli
½ tbsp lemon zest, finely grated

60ml (*2.1fl oz*) lemon juice, plus 1 tbsp to garnish
½ tsp salt
1 tbsp groundnut oil
1 tbsp garlic, sliced
3 tbsp shallots, sliced

3 tbsp red Thai chillies, sliced
mussels, debearded
½ cup Thai basil leaves, roughly chopped
¼ cup micro coriander leaves

To prepare the dish, place the coconut milk, galangal, lemon grass and green chilli in a saucepan, and bring to the boil over a high heat. Add the lemon zest and lower the heat, letting the mixture simmer for 10 minutes.

Remove the pan from the heat and strain, pressing down on the mixture. Cool to room temperature, uncover and add the lemon juice and salt. Stir well to combine and set aside.

To cook the mussels, heat some oil in a saucepan. Add the garlic and shallots and cook until lightly browned. Stir in the chillies, then the mussels and the lemongrass infusion. Shake the pan vigorously, then add the basil and season to taste. Cover and cook until the mussels open, which should take roughly 3 minutes.

To serve, transfer the mussels to a warmed serving bowl, top with the cooking liquid and garnish with the coriander leaves.

	Florian Favario	*Celeste at The Lanesborough*	Roasted cauliflower with lemon curry infused oil and aged parmesan
	Antonio Favuzzi	*L'Anima*	Hand-made malloreddus with mazara prawns and bottarga
	Romuald Feger	*Four Seasons Hotel London at Park Lane*	Roasted venison loin with celeriac mousseline and cranberry marmalade
	Chanaka Fernando	*Buddha Bar*	Red monkfish thai curry with steamed rice, broccoli and daikon
	Neil Forbes	*Café St Honoré*	Crisp Loch Creran oysters with sauce gribiche
	Russell Ford	*108 Brasserie at The Marylebone*	Seared mackerel with warm potato salad, chorizo and mustard dressing
	Gary Foulkes	*Angler*	Steamed cornish turbot with line-caught squid and dashi
	Damien Fremont	*Gastronhome*	Roasted halibut fillet with Scottish mussels, white asparagus and grenobloise sauce
	Martin Gabler	*The Lowndes Bar & Kitchen*	Prawn spaghetti with chilli, tomato, garlic and lemon zest
	Daniel Galmiche	*The Gore Hotel*	Pan-roasted wild halibut with tomato confit, feta, rosemary crisps and aioli

Foodie fact #9
The tea bag was invented by
Thomas Sullivan in 1908.

Marcus Bean - *The Brompton Cookery School*
Chicken supremes in lovage butter en papillote
Unlock these 250 recipes on the free CHARITABLE BOOKINGS lifestyle app.

FABIO CUOFANO
Goat

SEA BASS with miso glaze, baby spinach, fennel, pomodori secchi
SERVES 1 | PREPARATION TIME 10 MINUTES | COOKING TIME 10 MINUTES

For the Dish

170g (*6oz*) fillet of sea bass, halved
5g (*0.2oz*) salt
5ml (*0.2fl oz*) rapeseed oil

40g (*1.4oz*) miso reduction
2g (*0.07oz*) sesame or poppy seeds
20g (*0.7oz*) pomodori secchi — mini sundried tomatoes

80g (*2.8oz*) baby spinach
30g (*1.1oz*) fennel
5g (*0.2oz*) basil oil
1g (*0.035oz*) micro basil leaves
2g (*0.07fl oz*) extra virgin olive oil

To prepare the fish, season the sea bass with salt and sear the fish on the skin-side. Pour the rapeseed oil into a pan on a very high heat and fry the sea bass skin-side down for 1.5 minutes. Finish in the oven on 220°C (*430°F*) in a baking tray for another 3 minutes.

Dress the plate by making a spiral of the miso glaze, then sprinkling the poppy or sesame seeds over the top. Place the pomodori secchi at intervals onto the glaze.

Cook the spinach on a low heat in a pan with virgin olive oil and place neatly in the middle of the plate.

Take the fennel and shave into slices, coating lightly in the basil oil and then place onto the spinach.

To serve, stack the sea bass on top and garnish with micro basil.

MARK DODSON
The Masons Arms

LOIN OF VENISON with poached pear and blue cheese gratin

SERVES 4 | PREPARATION TIME 1 HOUR | COOKING TIME 10 HOURS

For the Venison
4 x 150g (5.3oz) venison loin, trimmed, keep the bones and trimmings for sauce

For the Poached Pears
2 pears, peeled, halved and cored
200ml (7fl oz) red wine
100g (3.5oz) sugar
1 stick of cinnamon

For the Venison Sauce
venison bones and trimmings
2 carrots, chopped
1 onion, chopped
1 stick celery, chopped
1 tbsp tomato purée
2 tbsp pear poaching liquid
water, to cover

For the Blue Cheese Gratin
4 medium potatoes, peeled
90ml (3.2fl oz) full-fat milk
125ml (4.4fl oz) double cream
3 cloves of garlic
200g (7oz) blue cheese, preferably gorgonzola

To Serve
salsify
cavolo nero
baby carrots

To make the venison sauce, preheat the oven to 180°C (355°F). Roast the bones and trimmings for 45 minutes until golden brown before transferring into a smaller pan with the vegetables. Add a spoonful of tomato purée, sweat again, then cover with water. Leave the mixture to cook slowly for 8 hours. Once cooked, pass through a fine sieve and reduce until a good sauce consistency is achieved. Just before serving, reduce a couple of spoonfuls of the pear poaching liquid and add to the sauce to give a little depth and sweetness.

To make the blue cheese gratin, preheat the oven to 150°C (300°F). Boil the milk, cream, garlic and cheese together. Slice the potatoes and position in a suitable dish, pour the liquid over the slices. Cover the top of the dish with greaseproof paper and bake in the oven for 1-1.5 hours. Halfway through cooking, press down on the potatoes to ensure the gratin is compact, the potato should have a good colour but be soft all the way through.

To make the poached pears, poach in the red wine with sugar and the cinnamon stick until just cooked. Leave them to cool in the liquid.

To serve, cook the venison in a pan until pink and leave to rest before slicing. Cook the vegetables as desired. Arrange the meat on the plate with the vegetables and add a good piece of the gratin. Slice and fan the pear before finally pouring a little of the sauce around the dish.

Jeff and Chris Galvin	*Galvin Restaurants*	Fillet of John Dory with orange glazed endive
Graham Garrett	*The West House*	Warm smoked haddock with bacon dressing and pea shoots
Laurie Gear	*Artichoke*	Saddle of Chiltern venison with caramelised shallots, salt-baked celeriac, hawthorn berry and rosehip emulsion, and venison sauce
Hari Ghotra	*Tamarind Collection of Restaurants*	Baked whole head of cauliflower drenched in a creamy mughlai gravy
Oliver Gladwin	*Nutbourne*	Cheek to tail Sussex beef and Madera jus
Yahir Gonzalez	*Aqua Nueva*	Cod, lardo, fennel
Peter Gordon	*The Providores and Tapa Room*	Lamb neck with baked pitta, figs, feta, tomato, cucumber, mint and kalamata olives
Joe Gould	*Fishmore Hall*	Pork tenderloin with carrot quinoa, smoked ginger, nashi pear, braised pork cheek
Ioannis Grammenos	*The Hippodrome Casino*	USDA prime meatballs with mushroom sauce
Jose Graziosi	*Hotel Endsleigh*	Lobster and turbot with new potatoes, caviar, sea vegetables and beurre blanc

Foodie fact #10
Almonds are members of the peach family.

Galton Blackiston - *Morston Hall*
Crab toasties with potato-wrapped quails' eggs
Unlock these 250 recipes on the free CHARITABLE **BOOKINGS** lifestyle app.

STEVEN DOHERTY
The First Floor Cafe

CULLEN SKINK

SERVES 4 | PREPARATION TIME 20 MINUTES | COOKING TIME 1 HOUR

For the Cullen Skink
2 large potatoes, washed, peeled and cut into 6 even pieces
salt and ground white pepper
1l (35fl oz) water
125ml (4.4fl oz) milk

2 tbsp onion, finely diced
4 x 125g (4.4oz) smoked haddock fillets, deskinned and pin boned
125g (4.4oz) leeks, split lengthways, washed and finely sliced

125g (4.4oz) savoy cabbage, quartered, washed and finely sliced
For the Garnish
parsley, chopped or picked
soft poached egg, optional

To make the cullen skink, put the potatoes into a pan of cold water with a teaspoon of salt. Bring to a simmer and allow to cook for 15 minutes. In a large pan, add the litre of cold water, the milk and onion and bring to a simmer. Add the fish and cook for 5 minutes. Remove the fish with a slotted spoon onto a clean plate, cover with cling film and keep warm. Add the leeks and cabbage to the cooking liquid and cook for a further 7 minutes. Drain the potatoes and mash until smooth. Stir enough mash into the leeks and cabbage to thicken the broth. Taste for seasoning, you may need to add a little pepper.

To serve, you can either flake the haddock and stir into the broth, or put the haddock into a deep soup plate and pour the broth over it. Either way, garnish with parsley and top with a soft-poached egg if desired.

ANDREW DU BOURG
The Elderflower

BLACK SHEEP with caramelised cauliflower and roast root vegetables

SERVES 2 | PREPARATION TIME 1 HOUR + 12 HOURS TO MARINATE | COOKING TIME 8 HOURS

For the Dish
1 rack of mutton, French trimmed
40ml (*1.4fl oz*) veal glaze
50ml (*1.8fl oz*) squid ink
20ml (*0.7fl oz*) soy sauce
30g (*1.1oz*) tomato ketchup
20g (*0.7oz*) roast garlic purée
1 large sprig of mint, rosemary and thyme
10 black peppercorns
80g (*2.8oz*) salted anchovies
2 cans Coca-Cola
1l (*35fl oz*) chicken stock

For the Cauliflower Purée
1 cauliflower
double cream, to cover
salt and pepper

For the Root Vegetables
selection of root vegetables
rapeseed oil, drizzle of
2 sprigs of thyme, picked
2 cloves of garlic
rock salt

To prepare the mutton, put all the liquid ingredients together with the mint, rosemary, peppercorns, garlic purée and anchovies into a blender and blitz. Pour over the French trimmed racks of mutton and marinate for 12 hours.

Preheat the oven to 85°C (*185°F*) and cook the mutton for 8 hours. Remove from the oven and allow the meat to cool in the sauce. Then remove the meat and reduce the sauce to a glazing consistency.

To prepare the caramelised cauliflower purée, remove the florets and place in a roasting tray. Drizzle with rapeseed oil and roast at 180°C (*355°F*) until nice and golden brown. Place in a food processor, add seasoning and cover with double cream. Blitz until smooth and season with salt and pepper to taste.

To prepare the root vegetables, neatly cut them into nice cubes. Drizzle with rapeseed oil, picked thyme, cloves of garlic and rock salt. Roast at 180°C (*355°F*) until caramelised and soft to touch.

	Andrew Green	*The Lowry Hotel*	Slow cooked Cheshire beef fillet with mustard crust, butternut squash purée, girolles and beef jus
	Mark Greenaway	*Restaurant Mark Greenaway*	Roasted wild salmon and cucumber
	Hywel Griffith	*Beach House*	Tandoori spiced cod with leek, spring onions and capers
	Marcel Grzyb	*Galley*	Sea bass with gnocchi, wild mushrooms, peas and truffle
	Simon Gueller	*The Box Tree*	Stuffed pigs trotters
	William Guthrie	*Buckland Manor*	Pan fried John Dory with spring garden vegetables and maple cured bacon
	Adam Handling	*The Frog Restaurant*	Chicken and lobster yellow curry
	Anna Hansen	*The Modern Pantry*	Salmon with a black garlic, liquorice and macadamia crust, and tomatillo salsa
	Marc Hardiman	*Great Fosters*	Native lobster risotto with shellfish, plankton and dill
	Angela Hartnett	*Murano*	Hake with Romesco crust

Foodie fact #11
Peanuts are legumes, not nuts.

Pedro Miranda - *Four Degree*
Saffron miso black cod with kohlrabi purée, razor clam, sea spray
Unlock these 250 recipes on the free CHARITABLE **BOOKINGS** lifestyle app.

SAM DUNLEAVY
Eastway Brasserie

ROAST GRESSINGHAM DUCK with caramelised carrot purée, roast carrots and fig jus
SERVES 4 | PREPARATION TIME 30 MINUTES | COOKING TIME 1 HOUR

For the Duck
4 duck breasts
salt and pepper
For the Pan-Fried Carrots
12 baby carrots

For the Caramelised Carrot Purée
500g (*18oz*) carrots
1 pinch of salt
150g (*5.3oz*) butter

For the Fig Jus
1l (*35fl oz*) beef stock
100g (*3.5oz*) dried figs
salt and pepper
For the Garnish
coriander cress

To make the caramelised carrot purée, remove the tops and tails and peel the large carrots. Roughly chop them and place in a saucepan, covering with water and a pinch of salt. Cook the carrots until soft, approximately 30–40 minutes. Whilst the carrots are cooking, add the butter to a saucepan and place on the stove. Cook on a medium heat until the milk solids separate from the butter. Skim the foam off the surface and wait for the remaining butter to turn golden brown with a nutty aroma. Once cooked, drain, keeping some of the liquid for the purée. Place the cooked carrots in a blender with the brown butter and blend, adding a little bit of the carrot cooking liquid if the purée is too thick. Season to taste and set to one side.

To prepare the fig jus, reduce 1l (*35fl oz*) of beef stock down to 300ml (*10.6fl oz*) and add the dried figs, allowing them to rehydrate and flavour the sauce.

To cook the roast duck, remove the duck breast from the fridge 20 minutes before cooking. Trim any excess fat from the duck and season the breasts with salt and pepper. Cook on each side for 2 minutes in a hot pan, then place in an oven at 170°C (*340°F*) for 5 minutes. Once cooked, let the meat rest for a further 5 minutes to achieve the perfect, pink duck.

To finish the dish and serve, quickly fry the baby carrots in the same pan as the duck, constantly turning them until they are nicely golden brown. Plate as pictured, covering the base of the plate with purée and topping with duck and baby carrots. Garnish with coriander cress and cover generously in fig jus.

DEAN EDWARDS
Celebrity Chef

CHICKEN AND CHORIZO LASAGNE

SERVES 4 | PREPARATION TIME 15 MINUTES | COOKING TIME 1 HOUR

For the Lasagne
4–5 chicken thighs, skinless and boneless
100g (3.5oz) chorizo, cubed
1 tbsp olive oil
1 large onion, very finely diced
2 sticks of celery, finely diced
1 tbsp thyme, chopped
3 cloves of garlic, crushed

150ml white wine
½ tsp smoked paprika
2 x 400g (14oz) cans of chopped tomatoes
1 tsp sugar
sea salt and black pepper,
8–9 fresh lasagne pasta sheets
70g (2.5oz) cheddar cheese, grated

For the White Sauce
50g (1.8oz) unsalted butter
50g (1.8oz) plain flour
500ml (18fl oz) milk

To prepare the filling, put the chicken thighs in a food processor and pulse until they are broken down. Don't over process though, as it's nice to have a few slightly larger pieces in the mixture. Add a dash of oil to a non-stick frying pan, tip in the chicken mince and brown over a medium to high heat. Remove the chicken from the pan and set aside.

Using the same pan with a little more oil if you need it, cook the chorizo, onion, celery, thyme and garlic for 5 minutes until softened. Add the wine and continue to cook until the liquid is reduced by half. Put the chicken back in the pan and add the paprika and tomatoes, then reduce the heat to a simmer and cook for 20 minutes. Season with the sugar, salt and pepper.

To make the white sauce, melt the butter over a medium heat. Whisk in the flour and cook for 2 minutes, stirring constantly. Pour in the milk and continue whisking until it comes to a boil, then reduce the heat and simmer the sauce for 5 minutes, stirring occasionally, then season.

Preheat the oven to 200°C (390°F). Grease an ovenproof dish measuring about 33x23cm (13x9in). Spread a thin layer of chicken sauce in the bottom of the dish, then add a sheet of lasagne, then more chicken sauce. Add another sheet of pasta, followed by white sauce, then the chicken sauce. Continue until everything is used up, finishing with a layer of white sauce. Sprinkle with cheese and bake in the oven for 40 minutes.

Prahlad Hegde	*Bombay Brasserie*	Masala sea bass
Matt Hide	*Turf Club*	Pan-fried sea bass with crushed jersey royals, asparagus, tomato and red onion salsa
Matt Hill	*Down Hall Country House Hotel*	Salt-Baked beetroot with Jersey Curd and pickled walnuts
Nathan Hill	*Orestone Manor*	Noisette of lamb with herb crust, navet purée, wild garlic, pomme fondant and rosemary jus
Hideki Hiwatashi	*Sake no Hana*	Sea bass with champagne yuzu miso sauce
Luke Holder	*Hartnett Holder & Co at Lime Wood*	Polenta agnolotti with artichokes, tomatoes and truffle
Sebby Holmes	*Farang*	Khao Soi - Chiang Mai curried egg noodles with barbecue butternut squash
Ken Hom	*Celebrity Chef*	Savoury beef with asparagus
Clive Howe	*Garrick Club*	Garrick game pie with wild mushrooms
Dan Howes	*The Gilbert Scott*	Grilled Iberico pork with Romesco

Foodie fact #12
Honey is not the only foodstuff that lasts forever. salt, sugar, oats, vinegar and raw rice also have eternal shelf lives.

Dave Mothersill - *The Salt Room*
Hake with cider, seaweed, mussels and artichokes
Unlock these 250 recipes on the free CHARITABLE BOOKINGS lifestyle app.

FLORIAN FAVARIO

Celeste at The Lanesborough

ROASTED CAULIFLOWER with lemon curry infused oil and aged Parmesan

SERVES 4 | PREPARATION TIME 15 MINUTES | COOKING TIME 30 MINUTES

For the Cauliflower
1 cauliflower
100g (3.5oz) onion
50g (1.8oz) tempura mix
200ml (7fl oz) milk
200ml (7fl oz) single cream

For the Curry Dressing
1 tsp curry powder
150ml (5.3fl oz) olive oil
30ml (1.1fl oz) lemon juice
½ tsp salt

To Serve
coriander cress, for decoration
aged Parmesan, grated

To make the cauliflower, start by cutting all the florets off of the stem. Keep the four largest florets to the side for the garnish, utilising the rest for the purée. Add the four larger florets to a pot of salted, boiling water and cook for 8 minutes. Immediately chill in ice water. Once cold, remove and leave to drain.

To make the cauliflower purée, finely slice the smaller florets and place in a saucepan with a pinch of salt. Sweat them for 6 minutes on a low heat then add the milk and cream. Cook for 20 minutes on a medium heat, then blend to a purée. Pass through a fine chinois.

To make the curry dressing, mix all the ingredients together.

To prepare the tempura onion, make the tempura mix, whisking together the tempura and a little water until a creamy consistency is reached. Slice the onion into half centimetre thick slices, dip in the tempura mix and fry until crispy.

To serve, dress the plate with the cauliflower purée and a handful of chopped tempura onion. Fry the cauliflower florets until golden brown. Add the cauliflower on top of the purée and drizzle with curry oil. At the last moment, sprinkle with coriander cress, top with grated aged Parmesan and serve.

NEIL FORBES
Café St Honoré

CRISP LOCH CRERAN OYSTERS with sauce gribiche

SERVES 4 | PREPARATION TIME 20 MINUTES | COOKING TIME 5 MINUTES

For the Oysters
16-24 oysters, allow 4-6
oysters per person
1 tbsp plain flour, seasoned
with salt and pepper
1 egg, beaten with a splash
of milk
1 handful of breadcrumbs
2 tbsp cold-pressed rapeseed
oil for shallow frying

For the Sauce Gribiche
1 hard-boiled egg, white and
yolk chopped separately
4 tbsp mayonnaise
1 shallot, peeled and finely
chopped
1 tbsp cornichons and capers,
chopped
1 tbsp chopped parsley and
tarragon
lemon juice, squeeze of
salt and pepper

To Serve
fennel fronds for garnish
coarse sea salt mixed with a
little water, as a bed for the
oyster shells

To prepare the oysters, be very careful not to puncture the oyster flesh when removing them from their shells. Ask your fishmonger to do this for you if you prefer, but make sure you keep the shells and clean thoroughly for serving. Roll each oyster through the flour, then the egg wash, then breadcrumbs and set to one side.

For the sauce gribiche, gently mix the chopped egg and mayonnaise, then add the shallot, cornichons, capers, parsley and tarragon, and a splash of lemon juice and season with salt and pepper. Mix together gently.

Place a frying pan on the hob and bring it to a medium heat before adding the oil. Once the oil is hot, gently cook the oysters, being careful not to burn them. Turn them often and cook for a minute or so either side. Remove the oysters from the pan and dab them with kitchen paper.

To serve, place the wet salt on a serving dish, arranging the oyster shells on top. Return the cooked oysters to the shells, placing a dot of sauce gribiche and a frond of fennel on top of each. Eat immediately.

	Louis Kenji Huang	*Oliver Maki*	Forest haze salad
	Chad Hughes	*The Lawns at Thornton Hall Hotel*	Poached turbot with wasabi sauce, wasabi foam, pickled cucumber and tenderstem broccoli
	Tom Hunter	*The Scarlet*	Ox cheek ragout with saffron pasta, mushrooms and parmesan
	Walter Ishizuka	*Brasserie Joel*	Honey and soy sauce glazed black cod with verbena pea purée and cider vinegar roasted peaches
	Gary Jones	*Belmond Le Manoir aux Quat'Saisons*	Lobster plancha with red pepper jus and cardamom
	Judy Joo	*Jinjuu Restaurant*	Korean roasted pork belly bossam
	Martijn Kajuiter	*House at the Cliff House Hotel*	Lamb rack loin with sweetbread, broad beans, goats cheese souffle and gremolata
	Jonas Karlsson	*100 Wardour St*	Roasted duck breast with savoy cabbage and parsnip
	Hanan Kattan	*Tabun Kitchen*	Lamb three ways
	Jacob Kenedy	*Bocca Di Lupo*	Orecchiette with Nduja

Foodie fact #13
Broccoli contains twice the
vitamin C of an orange.

Greg **Newman** - *The Jackrabbit Restaurant at The Kings Hotel*
Roasted cornish cod loin with heritage cauliflowers and smoked raisins
Unlock these 250 recipes on the free CHARITABLE **BOOKINGS** lifestyle app.

GARY FOULKES

Angler

STEAMED CORNISH TURBOT with line-caught squid and dashi

SERVES 4 | PREPARATION TIME 20 MINUTES | COOKING TIME 5 MINUTES

For the Dish
100g (3.5oz) nameko mushrooms
100g (3.5oz) golden enoki mushrooms
100g (3.5oz) white shimeji mushrooms
100g (3.5oz) brown shimeji mushrooms
25g (0.9oz) sliced, cleaned squid
4 x 120g (4.2oz) portions of Cornish turbot
1 pinch of salt
100g (3.5oz) rock samphire
80g (2.8oz) monk's beard
1 spritz of lemon juice

For the Dashi
375ml (13.2fl oz) water
35ml (1.2fl oz) soy sauce
20ml (0.7fl oz) mirin
9g (0.3oz) bonito flakes
9g (0.3oz) wakame flakes

Snip the caps off the mushrooms with a small pair of scissors and put to one side. Thinly slice the fresh squid and keep in the fridge. Place the turbot on a piece of greaseproof paper on a tray and lightly season with salt. Steam the turbot for 4 minutes or until cooked.

In the meantime, poach the mushrooms in a small amount of the dashi until they are just cooked. This should take around 3 minutes. Drop in the samphire and then the squid. Quickly blanch the monk's beard in some boiling, salted water and dress with lemon juice. Put to one side.

Place the mushrooms in a bowl and carefully set the steamed turbot fillet on the top. Place the monk's beard on top of the fish.

To make the dashi, bring the water to the boil and add in all the other ingredients and leave the mixture to infuse for 10 minutes.

Serve immediately with a little of the dashi on the side.

IOANNIS GRAMMENOS

The Hippodrome Casino

USDA PRIME MEATBALLS with mushroom sauce

SERVES 4 | PREPARATION TIME 45 MINUTES | COOKING TIME 1 HOUR

For the Meatballs
800g (28oz) USDA prime beef, freshly minced
2 tbsp olive oil
50g (1.8oz) shallots, finely chopped
10g (0.35oz) garlic, freshly chopped
10g (0.35oz) parsley, freshly chopped
6g (0.2oz) fresh oregano, finely chopped

1 free range egg, beaten
10g (0.35oz) salt and freshly ground pepper
For the Mushroom Sauce
150g wild forest mushrooms, sliced
1 tbsp olive oil or butter
1 small shallot, finely chopped
1 clove of garlic, crushed
10g dried porcini, soaked in 50ml (1.8fl oz) water
200ml (7fl oz) fresh double cream

salt and pepper
500ml (18fl oz) olive oil to fry meatballs
1 tbsp olive oil or butter
1 small shallot, finely chopped
1 clove of garlic, crushed
10g dried porcini, soaked in 50ml (1.8fl oz) water
200ml (7fl oz) fresh double cream
salt and pepper
500ml (7fl oz) olive oil to fry the meatball

To prepare the meatballs, heat two tablespoons of the olive oil in a heavy saucepan over a medium heat and add the shallots and garlic. Sweat for a few minutes until soft and golden. Allow to cool. In a mixing bowl, add the USDA prime minced beef with the cold, sweated shallots and garlic. Add the chopped parsley, oregano, and the beaten egg. Season the mixture with salt and pepper. Fry a bit of the mixture to check the seasoning and adjust if necessary. Divide the mixture into 16 round balls, cover and refrigerate.

To make the mushroom sauce, heat the oil or butter in a medium saucepan over a medium heat and add the shallot and garlic until golden. Add the wild mushrooms and the porcini and cook until lightly browned. Add the 50ml of water from the porcini and cook until reduced. Add the cream, salt and pepper and bring to the boil. Cook for 6-8 minutes, stirring occasionally, making sure that the cream doesn't over boil. Once the sauce has reduced by half, remove it from the heat and blend in a food processor until creamy and smooth.

To cook the meatballs, heat a frying pan and cook the meatballs for about 8-10 minutes in olive oil.

To serve, plate the meatballs and cover with mushroom sauce.

	Daniel Kent	*Wiltons*	Wiltons' roast grouse
	Jude Kereama	*Kota*	Nori wrapped cornish hake with mussels, cockles, seaweed, crispy rock shrimp, crab ravioli and dashi
	Tom Kerridge	*The Hand and Flowers*	Rump steak stew
	Justin Kett	*The Swan at Lavenham*	Venison and autumn vegetables
	Ronnie Kimbugwe	*Bel & The Dragon*	Salt-baked saddle of lamb
	Tom Kitchin	*The Kitchin*	Shellfish rockpool
	Atul Kochhar	*Benares*	Chana ghosht lamb rump with chickpeas
	Anthony Kong	*Le Chinois at The Millennium Knightsbridge*	Breadcrumb fried chicken thighs with fresh honey and lime sauce
	Pranee Laurillard	*Giggling Squid*	Thai chicken red curry
	Jeremy Lee	*Quo Vadis*	Smoked eel sandwich

Foodie fact #14
Rice is the primary staple food for over half the world's population.

Mark Potts - *The Mount Somerset Hotel and Spa*
Duck breasts
Unlock these 250 recipes on the free CHARITABLE BOOKINGS lifestyle app.

HYWEL GRIFFITH

Beach House

TANDOORI SPICED COD with leek, spring onions and capers

SERVES 4 | PREPARATION TIME 1 HOUR | COOKING TIME 2 HOURS 30 MINUTES

For the Tandoori Spiced Cod
1kg (2.2lb) cod
50g (1.8oz) salt
tandoori powder, to dust
1 drizzle of vegetable oil

For the Leek Purée
1kg (2.2kg) leeks
20ml (0.7fl oz) vegetable oil
1 pinch of salt
¼ tsp xanthan gum

For the Tandoori Butter
10g (0.35oz) tandoori powder
100g (3.5oz) butter
1 lemon, juiced

For the Garnish
4 spring onions
1 handful capers
vegetable oil to fry
200ml (7fl oz) almond milk
½ tsp lecithin
salt and pepper

To prepare the tandoori spiced cod, scale the fish, remove all the bones, salt the fish and leave for 1 hour. Wash thoroughly and pat dry. Cut the cod into 4 pieces and dust generously with the tandoori powder. Heat a little oil in a frying pan and cook the cod, skin-side down, for 3 minutes until crispy. Turn the cod over and allow to rest for 2 minutes off the heat.

Slice the leeks, wash thoroughly, then drain well. Place in a heavy-bottomed pan with the oil and a pinch of salt, then cook until the leeks are completely dry. The pan will catch and colour the leeks, this is perfectly fine. Blend with the xanthan gum to help smooth and stabilise the purée. Pass through a fine chinois.

Make the tandoori butter by dry frying the spices in a hot pan. Next add the butter, cook until nut brown and finish with the lemon juice.

For the garnish, thinly slice the spring onions, cover with cold water and refrigerate for 2 hours to make crisp. Fry the drained capers in hot oil until crispy. Place on a cloth to absorb any excess oil. Combine the lecithin with the warmed almond milk, season and use a hand blender to froth.

To serve, place the purée into the bowls, set the cod on top, then dress with the tandoori butter and garnishes.

ANGELA HARTNETT

Murano

HAKE with romesco crust

SERVES 4 | PREPARATION TIME 20 MINUTES | COOKING TIME 2 HOURS

For the Dish

1 x 290g (*10.2oz*) jar roasted red peppers, drained and quartered
1 tbsp fresh rosemary leaves, chopped

2 cloves of garlic, thinly sliced
3 tbsp olive oil
50g (*1.8oz*) skinned, salted almonds
50g (*1.8oz*) dry white breadcrumbs

2 medium courgettes
4 x 150g (*5.3oz*) hake portions, skin on
salt and freshly ground black pepper

Preheat the oven to 100°C (*212°F*), lay the peppers on a baking sheet and sprinkle with the rosemary, garlic, 1 tablespoon of olive oil and some seasoning. Place in the oven and bake for 2 hours to dry out the peppers. Remove from the oven and allow to cool. Once cool, place the peppers in a food processor with the almonds and breadcrumbs and blend until they have a sandy texture.

Increase the oven temperature to 180°C (*355°F*).

Slice the courgettes into discs 5mm thick. Heat 1 tablespoon of olive oil in a non-stick frying pan, add the courgettes and season. Cook for 2–3 minutes on each side or until golden. Remove from the pan and set aside.

Heat the remaining 1 tablespoon of olive oil in the frying pan over a high heat. Add the hake portions, skin-side down, and cook for 2 minutes, or until the skin is golden brown.

Transfer to a baking sheet, skin-side up, and sprinkle the prepared topping over the fish. Bake in the oven for 5–7 minutes, or until the flesh offers no resistance when you pierce it with the tip of a knife.

To serve, place the courgettes on individual plates and top with a piece of hake. Finish by spooning over some of the cooking juices.

	Stefano Leone	*Sauterelle*	Pistachio crusted salt marsh lamb loin with salsify purée, must sauce and red chicory
	Tom Lewis	*Monachyle Mhor*	Monachyle venison with garden chard and Balquhidder chanterelles
	Lee Che Liang	*Park Chinois*	Cobia and chinese chive flower stir-fry
	Daren Liew	*Duddell's London*	Abalone rice with US asparagus and Hon Shimeji mushroom
	Jose Lopez	*Patérnoster Chop House*	Duck and bean casserole
	James Lowe	*Lyle's*	Saddleback loin with bitter leaves and burnt apple
	James Mackenzie	*The Pipe and Glass Inn*	Crab, carrot and coriander salad with toasted hazelnuts and sea salt flat bread
	Rob Malyon	*The Wright Brothers - Borough*	Beef and oyster pie
	Gregory Marchand	*Frenchie*	Skate wing à la Grenobloise with seaweed
	Anthony Marshall	*The Hilton on Park Lane*	Beef fillet with celeriac purée, pickled onions, baby vegetables, ceps and thyme jus

Foodie fact #15
We humans share 60% of our DNA with bananas.

Glynn **Purnell** - *Purnell's*
Monkfish masala with red lentils, pickled carrots and coconut
Unlock these 250 recipes on the free CHARITABLE **BOOKINGS** lifestyle app.

PRAHLAD HEGDE

Bombay Brasserie

MASALA SEA BASS

SERVES 4 | PREPARATION TIME 20 MINUTES | COOKING TIME 20 HOUR

For the Dish
2 tsp chilli powder
2 tsp turmeric
1 lime, juiced
salt
4 x 180g (6.3oz) Chilean sea
bass, deboned, skin on
2 tbsp vegetable oil

For the Base
1 tbsp vegetable oil
4 tsp cumin
1 clove of garlic, chopped
80g (2.8oz) mushrooms, sliced
200g (7oz) baby spinach,
shredded
1 pinch of salt

For the Garnish
4 chilli flowers, made using
fresh
green or red chilli
4 chives
a few drops of chilli oil
4 lemon wedges

To make the dish, in a bowl, mix the chilli powder, turmeric and lime juice and season with salt. Spoon this over the sea bass. Set aside for 20 minutes to marinate. Preheat the oven to 180°C (355°F). Heat the vegetable oil in a pan and sear the marinated sea bass on both sides. Place on a tray and bake in the oven for 5 minutes.

To make the spinach and mushroom base, heat the oil in a pan, add the cumin and chopped garlic, and fry until the garlic turns golden brown. Add the mushrooms and shredded spinach and stir-fry until cooked. Season with salt.

To prepare the chilli flowers, snip off the tip of a fresh red or green chilli, leaving the stalk intact, and then make a few lengthways cuts at the snipped end. Place the chilli in ice water – after a while the ends will curl up like flowers.

To serve, divide the spinach and mushroom mixture among 4 large plates. On each base, place a sea bass fillet, skin-side up, and garnish with a chilli flower, a chive and a lemon wedge. Drizzle a few drops of chilli oil or a sprinkle of paprika powder on the plate.

KEN HOM
Celebrity Chef

SAVOURY BEEF with asparagus

SERVES 4 | PREPARATION TIME 15 MINUTES | COOKING TIME 30 MINUTES

For the Beef

450g (*15.9oz*) lean beef steak
450g (*15.9oz*) fresh asparagus
3 tbsp groundnut oil
100g (*3.5oz*) onions, thinly sliced
2 tbsp black beans, coarsely chopped
1½ tbsp garlic, finely chopped
2 tsp ginger, finely chopped

3 tbsp home-made or good-quality bought chicken stock or water
1 tbsp Shaoxing rice wine or dry sherry
1 tsp sugar
1½ tsp salt
½ tsp pepper
2 tbsp oyster sauce

For the Marinade

2 tsp light soy sauce
2 tsp Shaoxing rice wine or dry sherry
2 tsp sesame oil
2 tsp cornflour
½ tsp salt
¼ tsp pepper

Put the beef in the freezer for 20 minutes. This will allow the meat to harden slightly for easier cutting. Cut it into thin slices, each 4cm long. Put the beef slices in a bowl and add all of the marinade ingredients. Mix well and let the slices steep in the marinade for 15 minutes. Meanwhile, slice the asparagus on the diagonal into 7.5cm pieces and set aside until needed.

Heat a wok or large frying pan over a high heat until it is very hot. Add the oil and when it is very hot and slightly smoking, add the beef from the marinade and stir-fry for about 2 minutes. Remove the meat and drain it in a colander. Pour off all but approximately 1 tablespoons of the oil and reheat it over a high heat. When it is very hot, add the onions, black beans, garlic and ginger and stir-fry for 1 minute then add the asparagus and stir-fry for 1 minute. Now add the stock or water, rice wine or sherry, sugar, salt and pepper. Continue to stir-fry for 3 minutes or until the asparagus is slightly tender. Add more water as necessary.

Quickly return the meat to the wok, add the oyster sauce and stir well. Turn the mixture onto a warm platter and serve at once.

	Luke Matthews	*Chewton Glen*	New Forest venison poivrade with polenta chips, roasted root vegetables and blueberry sauce
	Robert Mazur	*Heddon Street Kitchen*	Slow roasted Cumbrian saddleback pork belly with braeburn apple purée and griotte onion
	Francesco Mazzei	*Sartoria*	Stracciatella ricotta tortelli
	Dave McCarthy	*Scott's*	Scott's roasted cod with arrocina beans, chorizo and padrón peppers
	Pip McCormac	*Author of cook book*	Lemon and herb spaghetti
	Ryan McCutcheon	*Greywalls Hotel*	Pan-seared North Atlantic halibut with mussel and clam gratin with sweet cider sauce and sauce rouille
	Enda McEvoy	*Loam*	Carrots with buttermilk and nasturtium
	Aidan McGee	*Corrigan's Mayfair*	Agnolotti, burrata, aubergine and courgette
	David Mcintyre	*CUT at 45 Park Lane*	Butter lettuce salad
	Peter McKenna	*The Gannet*	Scotch beef diamond muscle with ayrshire beets, artichoke, shallot, broccoli and madeira sauce

Foodie fact #16
There are around 2,000 different plant types that humans cultivate to use in food.

Damien Rigollet - *Coq d'Argent*
Cote de veau with creamy wild mushrooms and apples
Unlock these 250 recipes on the free CHARITABLE **BOOKINGS** lifestyle app.

DAN HOWES
The Gilbert Scott

GRILLED IBERICO PORK with romesco
SERVES 4 | PREPARATION TIME 30 MINUTES | COOKING TIME 1 HOUR 30 MINUTES

For the Dish
600g (21.2oz) Iberico pork secreto
For the Romesco Sauce
100g (3.5oz) piquillo peppers
6g garlic (0.2oz)
10ml (3.5fl oz) Cabernet Sauvignon vinegar
6g (0.2oz) sugar
3g (0.11oz) salt

2g (0.07oz) smoked paprika
20g (0.7oz) roasted almonds
20g (0.7oz) roasted hazelnuts
100g (3.5oz) crème fraîche, hung overnight in muslin cloth
For the Fennel
1 bulb of fennel
1 drizzle of olive oil
1 spritz of lemon juice
1 pinch of salt

For the Nduja Onions
200g (7oz) celeriac, peeled and cut into thin strips
400g (14oz) onions, thinly sliced
50g (1.8oz) nduja
10g (0.35oz) garlic, chopped
5g (0.18oz) sage
30ml (1.1fl oz) olive oil
1 bunch of grelot onions

To prepare the romesco sauce, blitz everything except the crème fraîche in a food processor until smooth then fold in the crème fraîche. Check the seasoning. To prepare the fennel, thinly slice the fennel and dress with some olive oil, lemon juice and salt.

To prepare the nduja onions, lightly salt the celeriac and put to one side. Put the rest of the ingredients in a covered pan and cook on a low heat for around 1 hour, remove the lid and allow some of the moisture to evaporate. Mix the onions with the celeriac and check the seasoning, keep warm.

To prepare the grelot onions, cut the onions in half and pan fry in a little olive oil.

To prepare the pork, season and grill over coal for a few minutes turning often. Allow to rest for a few minutes and slice.

To serve, assemble per the image shown.

HANAN KATTAN
Tabun Kitchen

LAMB THREE WAYS
SERVES 2 | PREPARATION TIME 30 MINUTES | COOKING TIME 30 MINUTES

For the Lamb Fillet
300g (*11oz*) lamb fillet, sliced or cubed
1 lemon, juiced
20ml (*0.7fl oz*) olive oil
1 tsp paprika
salt and pepper

For the Kofta Skewers
500g (*18oz*) minced lamb
70g (*2.5oz*) onion
150g (*5.3oz*) tahini
50g (*1.8oz*) chillies
100g (*3.5 oz*) parsley
5g (*0.18oz*) each salt and pepper
10g (*0.35oz*) each cinnamon, paprika and allspice

For the Kofta Balls
½ kofta mix, previously made
50g (*1.8oz*) green chilli, finely chopped
45g (*1.6oz*) parsley, finely chopped
100g (*3.5oz*) tahini
15g (*0.5oz*) pomegranate molasses

Marinate the lamb fillet slices or cubes in the oil, lemon, salt, pepper and paprika, and keep aside.

Mix all the kofta ingredients together. You can prepare this ahead of time and keep in the fridge for the flavours to absorb.

Divide the kofta mixture in half. One half can be formed around the skewers ready to grill.

To the other half of the kofta mix, add the chopped green chilli, parsley, tahini and pomegranate molasses. Form the mixture into 1.5cm round balls, and place them on a foil-covered tray. Place both the skewers and tahini balls under a very hot grill for 6-8 minutes, turning halfway through cooking.

To serve, pan fry the lamb for 2 minutes on each side, and plate as pictured.

	Brian Mcleish	*Moonfish Café*	Poached halibut with cauliflower, mussels, saffron and hazelnut
	Ben Mellor	*Blandford Comptoir*	Hake and artichoke barigoule
	Vincent Menager	*STK London*	Braised USDA beef short rib with bourbon glaze
	Pedro Miranda	*Four Degree*	Saffron miso black cod with kohlrabi purée, razor clam, sea spray
	Daniel Moon	*The Gainsborough Restaurant*	Roast breast of creedy carver duck and confit leg spring roll with plum purée and sesame seeds
	Maurizio Morelli	*Margot*	Stewed fillet of cod with courgettes, tomato and fresh herbs
	Anton Mosimann	*Mosimann's*	Pot-au-feu
	Dave Mothersill	*The Salt Room*	Hake with cider, seaweed, mussels and artichokes
	Yoshihiro Murata	*Tokimeitē*	Beef teriyaki
	Greg Newman	*The Jackrabbit Restaurant at The Kings Hotel*	Roasted cornish cod loin with heritage cauliflowers and smoked raisins

Foodie fact #17
The banana tree is not a true fruit tree at all but a
giant herb and the banana itself is actually it's berry.

Albert **Roux** - *Le Gavroche Cookbook*
Roast bresse pigeon with fresh peas
Unlock these 250 recipes on the free CHARITABLE BOOKINGS lifestyle app.

DANIEL KENT
Wiltons

WILTONS' ROAST GROUSE

SERVES 4 | PREPARATION TIME 30 MINUTES | COOKING TIME 1 HOUR

For the Grouse
1 grouse
20ml (*0.7fl oz*) sunflower oil
50g (*1.8oz*) diced celeriac, carrot and shallots
1 sprig of fresh thyme
1 dstp brandy

For the Gravy
200g (*7oz*) grouse trimmings
1 streaky bacon rasher
1 banana shallot, roughly diced
1 bulb of garlic, peeled and sliced
1 sprig of thyme
1 bay leaf
5 white peppercorns

salt, to taste
5 juniper berries
1 tsp sherry vinegar
1 tbsp port
1 tbsp red wine
500ml (*18fl oz*) veal stock
500ml (*18fl oz*) chicken stock
For the Garnish
2 streaky bacon slices

To make the roast gravy, colour off the grouse trimmings and bacon in a saucepan. Add the shallot, garlic, herbs and spices. Cook this on a medium heat for 5 minutes. Now add the sherry vinegar and let it reduce down to syrup. Keep stirring this to release any tasty morsels left on the pan. When it has become a syrup, add the port and reduce to a glaze. Add the red wine and reduce again to a thick syrup. Add the stocks and bring to the boil. Simmer, skim and cook out for about 40 minutes. Strain and place in the fridge until needed.

To cook the grouse, heat the oil in a heavy-duty pan that will just contain the grouse.

Lay the bird on one side of its breast and begin searing it. Turn it over on to the other side. Add the mirepoix and thyme. Turn it onto its back and continue to fry. Hold up the grouse and sear the plump ends of the breast. Pour the brandy into the pan. Transfer the pan with the grouse to a preheated oven at 200°C (*390°F*). Allow 8 minutes for medium rare and 12 minutes for medium. Rest the grouse at least 10 minutes before carving it.

To plate, carve the grouse and cover generously with reheated gravy, serving with all the trimmings.

GREGORY MARCHAND

Frenchie

SKATE WING A LA GRENOBLOISE with seaweed

SERVES 4 | PREPARATION TIME 15 MINUTES | COOKING TIME 15 MINUTES

For the Skate
4 skate wings, peeled and
trimmed seasoned flour, for
dredging
salt and pepper, to taste
2 tbsp butter
1 tbsp vegetable oil, for frying

For the Seaweed Grenobloise
50g (*1.8oz*) butter
2 tbsp capers, rinsed
½ cup croutons
2 lemons, 1 juiced, 1 segmented
1 cup mixed seaweeds, dulse,
sweet tangle, sea green, nori

To prepare the skate, put the flour in a shallow tray and dredge the fish in the flour.

Shake off the excess. Re-season the fish with salt and pepper.

To cook the skate, heat a sauté pan and melt 1 tablespoon of the butter and the vegetable oil over a medium-high heat. Once the butter is foaming, add the fish and cook for 2−3 minutes. Add the other tablespoon of butter, turn the fish and cook for a further 2−3 minutes. Transfer the fish to a warm platter.

To finish the dish, discard the butter from the pan and add the remaining 50g (*1.8oz*) butter.

Cook over a high heat until it gets foamy, then add the capers and croutons. Cook for 30 seconds, then add the lemon juice and seaweeds. Take off the heat and add the lemon segments. Season with salt and pepper, and spoon over the fish.

	Chantelle Nicholson	*Tredwells*	Duck with tamarind, cashew and fig
	Andrew Nutter	*Nutters Restaurant*	Pan-seared wild sea bass with jersey royal gratin and english asparagus with a chive and lemon hollandaise
	Malachi O'Gallagher	*The Delaunay*	Fillet of beef stroganoff
	Tom Oldroyd	*Oldroyd*	Grilled mackerel with beetroot, horseradish and salsa verde
	Robert Ortiz	*Lima*	Stone bass ceviche
	Dale Osborne	*Aqua Shard*	Loch Etive hot and cold smoked trout
	Jeremy Pang	*School of Wok*	Steamed wontons in chilli broth
	Antonina Parker	*Cook book author*	Mountain risotto with roast butternut squash and sage
	Tom Parker-Bowles	*Cookery Writer*	Tacos al carbon
	Aaron Patterson	*Hambleton Hall*	Truffle lasagne

Foodie fact #18
The first known soup was made from
hippopotamus and dates back to 6,000 B.C.

Martin Wishart - *Restaurant Martin Wishart*
Langoustine ravioli with braised orange endive and langoustine jus
Unlock these 250 recipes on the free CHARITABLE **BOOKINGS** lifestyle app.

FRANCESCO MAZZEI

Sartoria

STRACCIATELLA RICOTTA TORTELLI

SERVES 4 | PREPARATION TIME 1 HOUR 30 MINUTES | COOKING TIME 15 MINUTES

For the Pasta Dough
200g (7oz) 00 flour
200g (7oz) hard durum wheat flour
4 fresh eggs

For the Filling
500g (18oz) stracciatella di bufala
500g (18oz) ricotta
150g (5.3oz) Grana Padano Riserva
10g (0.35oz) truffle butter
egg yolk, to bind the pasta
salt and black pepper, to taste

For the Garnish
10 sage leaves
16 hazelnuts
200g (7oz) unsalted butter
a few drops of balsamic vinegar
microcress

To form the dough, mix the 2 flours together on the table, then make a hole in the middle. Put the eggs in the middle and mix slowly with the flour. The pasta needs to be kneaded by hand until it has a smooth surface. When the dough is ready, wrap it in cling film and store in the fridge for about an hour.

To prepare the filling, mix the stracciatella until the consistency is smooth. Add the ricotta cheese, 100g (3.5oz) of Grana Padano and a pinch of salt and pepper. Melt the truffle butter in a pan and add gradually to the mixture.

To make the tortelli, with a rolling pin, stretch out the dough into 1mm thick sheets, and cut it into 6—7cm squares. Put a little filling at the centre of each square, brush some egg yolk around the edges and close into a rectangular shape, making sure that the borders adhere well and no air is left inside.

Cook the tortelli in boiling water for approximately 3—4 minutes. In the meantime, melt the unsalted butter. Once it browns, add the sage and hazelnuts.

To serve, plate the tortelli and season with the brown butter and remaining grated Grana Padano. Drizzle with a few drops of balsamic vinegar and sprinkle with microcress.

ANTON MOSIMANN
Mosimann's

POT-AU-FEU

SERVES 4 | PREPARATION TIME 15 MINUTES | COOKING TIME 1 HOUR

For the Pot-Au-Feu
1 free range or organic chicken
2l (*3.5 pint*) white chicken stock
3 onions, peeled and each
studded with 2 cloves
1 bay leaf
2 cloves of garlic, peeled
a few white peppercorns
1 small bunch of mixed thyme,
rosemary and parsley

4 small carrots, peeled
4 pieces of celery, about 5cm
in length
4 pieces of leek, about 5cm in
length
8 small onions, peeled
1 small celeriac, peeled and
quartered
salt and freshly ground pepper

For the Garnish
flat leaf parsley, freshy chopped

To prepare the Pot-au-feu, bring a large saucepan of water to the boil. Add the chicken and bring back to the boil. Drain and allow to cook slightly.

In another large pan, boil the chicken stock with the onions, bay leaf, garlic, peppercorns and bunch of herbs. Simmer for 20 minutes. Add the chicken and poach for 20 minutes. Lift the chicken out of the pan. Strain the stock, absorb and remove the fat with strips of kitchen paper, then return the liquid to the cleaned out pan. Remove the skin from the chicken, then put it back in the pan with the stock. Add the vegetables. Bring to the boil and simmer for 10 minutes. Lift out the chicken and vegetables and keep warm. Boil the chicken stock rapidly to reduce by half. Adjust seasoning to taste.

To serve, carve the chicken and arrange in soup plates with the vegetables. Pour over some stock and garnish with parsley. Serve at once.

	Anne-Sophie Pic	*La Dame de Pic*	80-day matured Highland beef marinated in zacapa rum, phu quoc pepper and café Liberica de São Tomé, carrots and girolles
	Steve Pidgeon	*Arundell Arms*	Venison and chocolate casserole
	Alessio Piras	*Alberts Club*	Monkfish tail wrapped in Parma ham, sweet and sour peppers, samphire and caper dressing
	Mark Potts	*The Mount Somerset Hotel & Spa*	Duck breasts
	Alfred Prasad	*Tamarind*	Lamb shank curry
	Helena Puolakka	*Aster*	Pan seared hand dived scallops with sea buckthorn curd and crispy capers
	Glynn Purnell	*Purnell's*	Monkfish masala with red lentils, pickled carrots and coconut
	Juri Ravagli	*Brasserie at 1 Lombard Street*	Caramelised sablefish with vegetable spaghetti
	Roberto Reatini	*Ristorante Frescobaldi*	Veal chop with mashed potatoes and mushrooms
	Robert Reid	*Balthazar*	Duck shepherd's pie

Foodie fact #19
The word "companion" is derived from the Latin "com"
meaning "together" and "panis" meaning "bread".

Tim **Stamp** - *Ye Olde Bell*
Dexter beef fillet with maple glazed cured ham, grilled goat's cheese and baby root vegetables
Unlock these 250 recipes on the free CHARITABLE **BOOKINGS** lifestyle app.

YOSHIHIRO MURATA

Tokimeitē

BEEF TERIYAKI

SERVES 2 | PREPARATION TIME 10 MINUTES | COOKING TIME 15 MINUTES

For the Teriyaki
1½ tbsp sugar
3 tbsp soy sauce
6 tbsp sake

For the Beef
1 tbsp vegetable oil
2 x 100g (*3.5oz*) sirloin steaks
English mustard, to taste
sesame seeds, to taste
2 sprigs of watercress

To make the teriyaki sauce, mix together the soy sauce, sugar and sake, bring to the boil and reduce to a loose syrup.

Heat a frying pan over a medium high heat, add the oil and sear the steaks on both sides until browned. Lower the heat to medium. Add the teriyaki sauce and simmer. Shake the pan from time to time, basting the steaks with a spoon until the sauce thickens slightly and glazes the steaks. This should take approximately 4 minutes.

To serve, transfer the steaks to a cutting board and cut into 1.5cm thick slices. Arrange the steak slices on a serving plate and pour the sauce from the pan over. Sprinkle with the sesame seeds. Brush the English mustard at the base of the plate. Garnish the top of the plate with watercress.

ROBERT ORTIZ
Lima

STONE BASS CEVICHE
SERVES 2 | PREPARATION TIME 20 MINUTES

For the Leche De Tigre
100ml (*3.5fl oz*) fresh lime juice
2 cloves of garlic, smashed
1 tbsp fresh coriander leaves, chopped
20g (*0.7oz*) rocoto chilli, diced
100g (*3.5oz*) pink onions, sliced
salt, to taste

For the Ceviche
240g (*8.5oz*) stone bass, cut into even-sized pieces
100ml (*3.5fl oz*) leche de tigre
canchita
sweet potato glaze

For the Sweet Potato Glaze
2 large sweet potatoes, diced
50ml (*1.8fl oz*) mandarin juice
For the Garnish
micro amaranth, optional
reserved pink onion slices

To make the leche de tigre, blitz together the lime juice, garlic, coriander and rocoto chilli until smooth. Add the onions and blend again. Season to taste and chill.

To make the sweet potato glaze, cook the diced sweet potato in salted, boiling water and refresh in ice water. Blend to a purée with a little mandarin juice.

To assemble the ceviche, place the stone bass into a bowl. Season with a little salt and pour over the leche de tigre. Leave to marinate for approximately 2 minutes. Serve with the sweet potato glaze and canchita.

	Damien Rigollet	*Coq d'Argent*	Cote de veau with creamy wild mushrooms and apples
	Simon Rimmer	*TV Chef*	Saffron prawns with fennel
	Simon Rogan	*L'Enclume*	Grilled salad smoked over embers with isle of mull cheese, custard and cobnuts
	Albert Roux	*Le Gavroche*	Roast bresse pigeon with fresh peas
	Rupert Rowley	*Fischer's at Baslow Hall*	Goosnargh duck breast with fondant potato, garden vegetables and poached cherries
	Pasquale Russo	*Cotswold House*	Herb crusted hake fillet with pickled girolles, sea weed and coco beans
	Laura Santtini	*Santini Restaurant*	Truffled mac 'n' cheese
	Stefano Savio	*Quirinale*	Baked red mullet with taggiasche olives and tomato
	Andrew Scott	*Restaurant 56*	Coronation cornish crab with crab biscuit and panna cotta, apricot and almond
	Werner Seebach	*Chino Latino*	Slow cooked prime beef short rib with teriyaki sauce

Foodie fact #20
During the Middle Ages, a lemon slice was served with fish because it was thought the juice would dissolve any bones that were accidentally swallowed.

Jack **Stein** - *Rick Stein's*
Braised hake
Unlock these 250 recipes on the free CHARITABLE **BOOKINGS** lifestyle app.

JURI RAVAGLI
Brasserie at 1 Lombard Street

CARAMELISED SABLEFISH with vegetable spaghetti

SERVES 4 | PREPARATION TIME 10 MINUTES | COOKING TIME 15 MINUTES

Equipment
mandoline
For the Dish
1 banana leaf

For the Vegetable Spaghetti
2 green courgettes
2 yellow courgettes
2 carrots
4 pak choi

For the Caramelised Sablefish
4 x 200g (*7oz*) sablefish fillets - black cod, cleaned
400ml (*14fl oz*) soy sauce
160g (*5.6oz*) caster sugar
100ml (*3.5fl oz*) olive oil

Preheat the oven to 180°C (*355°F*).

Cut the banana leaf into 4 flat diamond shapes. Put a damp cloth on top to retain moisture and place to one side for later.

To prepare the vegetable spaghetti, take the courgettes and carrots and slice them with a mandoline, lengthways. Then with a knife, cut spaghetti like long, thin strands. Cut the pak choi in half, then blanch in salted boiling water for 2 minutes. Strain them and place in cold water, then dry them off using a cloth.

To make the caramelised sablefish, marinate the cod fillets in the soy sauce for a few minutes and then roll them in sugar. Place them in a preheated frying pan with a tablespoon of extra virgin olive oil, skin-side up. Gently cook until the base is caramelised. Repeat on the other side, then remove the fish from the frying pan. Add the remaining sugar and soy from the marinade to the pan. Let it boil for approximately 2 minutes. Place the fish on a baking tray lined with greaseproof paper and a little olive oil. Add the pak choi and pop in the oven for 5–6 minutes. In a separate pan, fry the vegetable spaghetti with 1 tbsp of olive oil, salt and pepper for approximately 2 minutes.

To serve, place a banana leaf diamond in the centre of each plate. Put the vegetable spaghetti on top, then layer the sablefish and pak choi. Dress the dish with the sweet soy sauce you prepared earlier and finish with a drizzle of extra virgin olive oil.

SIMON RIMMER
Celebrity Chef

SAFFRON PRAWNS with fennel

SERVES 2 | PREPARATION TIME 20 MINUTES

For the Prawns
1kg (*2.2lb*) king prawns, deveined, tail intact
200g (*7oz*) chickpea flour
15g (*0.53oz*) ground cumin
15g (*0.53oz*) ground coriander
5g (*0.18oz*) chilli flakes
7g (*0.25oz*) sea salt

For the Fennel
50ml (*1.8fl oz*) olive oil
3 red onions, cut into wedges
2 baby fennel bulbs, cut into wedges
8 strands of saffron, soaked in hot water for 30 minutes
20ml (*0.7fl oz*) red wine vinegar

15g (*0.53oz*) honey
6 plum tomatoes, each cut into 6 wedges
15g (*0.53oz*) golden raisins

For the Garnish
fresh mint, chopped
fresh coriander, chopped
fresh flat leaf parsley, chopped

To prepare the dish and cook the fennel, heat some oil in a large pan, cook the wedges of onion for 6 minutes, turning once a little charred. Add the fennel and cook for 4 minutes. Once coloured, add the saffron accompanied by the water it was soaked in, the honey, vinegar, plum tomato wedges and raisins. Cover and simmer for 20 minutes.

To cook the prawns, combine the flour, spices and salt. Toss the prawns in the mix, shake off any excess and deep fry for 2 minutes, preferably in 2 batches, until golden. Drain off any excess oil and set to one side ready for serving.

To serve, spoon some of the fennel mix into pasta bowls, top with the prawns and garnish with chopped mint, coriander and parsley.

	Ryan Shilton	*Four Seasons Restaurant at Swinfen Hall Hotel*	Wild sea bass with bacon emulsion, butternut squash, curried granola and sprouts
	Dan Shotton	*Yorebridge House*	Belly pork with Pan-fried squid and carrots
	Vivek Singh	*The Cinammon Club*	Rajasthani roast rump of lamb with corn sauce
	Joginder Singh Dham	*Butlers Wharf Chop House*	Braised lamb shank
	Geoffrey Smeddle	*The Peat Inn*	Pappardelle with shaved asparagus, broad beans, marjoram and pea purée
	Daniel Smith	*The Ingham Swan*	Destructed Cromer crab salad with blowtorched mackerel
	Scott Smith	*Norn*	Salt baked hogget with wild leeks and peasemeal
	Eric Snaith	*Titchwell Manor*	BBQ onion with potato gnocchi, avocado, brazil nuts and burnt onion crème fraîche
	Tim Stamp	*Ye Olde Bell*	Dexter beef fillet with maple glazed cured ham, grilled goat's cheese and baby root vegetables
	Jack Stein	*Rick's Café*	Braised hake

Foodie fact #21
The most expensive coffee in the world comes from civet poo!

Fernando Stovell - *Stovell's*
Foie gras with barbecue silverskin onions, toasted kentish cobnuts, hay dressing and nasturtium
Unlock these 250 recipes on the free CHARITABLE BOOKINGS lifestyle app.

STEFANO SAVIO
Quirinale

BAKED RED MULLET with Taggiasche olives and tomato
SERVES 2 | PREPARATION TIME 15 MINUTES | COOKING TIME 35 MINUTES

For the Tapenade
100g (3.5oz) Taggiasche olives, pitted
15g (0.53oz) capers, Pantellerian
10g (0.35oz) anchovies
½ clove of garlic
50g (1.8oz) breadcrumbs
micro organic sprouts and basil leaves, to serve

For the Tomato Sauce
50g (1.8oz) shallots
½ clove of garlic
200g (7oz) cherry tomatoes
1 tbsp extra virgin olive oil
salt and pepper
1 small bunch fresh basil

For the Mullet
2 x 400g (14oz) red mullets, filleted and head removed
6 chive stems, blanched

To make the tapenade, blend together the olives, capers, anchovies and half of the garlic clove in a food processor. Squeeze the paste through a muslin cloth and get rid of the excess liquid. Add the breadcrumbs to the paste and mix together.

Next make the tomato sauce. Sauté the shallots, the other half of the garlic and cherry tomatoes in a pan with some extra virgin olive oil, salt and pepper for about 20 minutes. Add the basil, then blend and pass through a sieve to obtain a smooth sauce.

Spread the tapenade between the two red mullet fillets. Tie the fillets together with the blanched chive, cut the fish in half and bake for about 7–8 minutes at 200°C (390°F).

To serve, spread the tomato sauce on a plate, lay the cooked mullet over it, and top with some basil leaves and micro organic sprouts.

ERIC SNAITH
Titchwell Manor

BBQ ONION with potato gnocchi, avocado, brazil nuts and burnt onion crème fraîche
SERVES 4 | PREPARATION TIME 20 MINUTES | COOKING TIME 1 HOUR

For the Onions
2 large white onions
100g (3.5oz) butter
1 tsp Maldon salt
150g (5.3oz) crème fraîche

For the Gnocchi
500g (18oz) King Edward potatoes
2 medium eggs, beaten
150g (5.3oz) 00 pasta flour
1 tbsp olive oil
1 pinch of salt

For the Avocado
1 ripe avocado
50g (1.8oz) crème fraîche
lemon juice and salt, to taste
To Finish
chopped brazil nuts
olive oil
1 knob of butter

Barbecue the onions with their skins on until black, allow to cool, then halve. Separate the flesh from the skins and retain both. Top the onion flesh with a knob of butter and the Maldon salt, then return with the skins to the barbecue. When the onion is soft, remove from the barbecue and keep aside until later. When the skins are black and crispy remove them also and allow to cool. Blitz the skins to a powder in a food processor and combine with the crème fraîche.

To prepare the gnocchi, boil the potatoes in salted water until just cooked, strain and pass through a potato ricer. Pass them through the ricer again onto a floured surface so that there are no lumps. Make a well in the middle, add the oil, eggs and flour and gently bring together into a dough but be careful not to overwork. Roll into finger size pieces and poach in salted water at just below boiling. When they float they are done. Drop them into ice water, then pat dry.

For the avocado, blitz it together with the crème fraîche until smooth. Mix with lemon juice and salt to taste.

To finish, place the onion in an oven at 180°C (355°F) until warmed through. Pan fry the gnocchi in a little olive oil on medium heat. When golden brown, add a knob of butter and allow to foam. Assemble as pictured.

	Rick Stein	*The Seafood Restaurant*	Steamed mussels with tomato and tarragon
	Fernando Stovell	*Stovell's*	Foie gras with barbecue silverskin onions, toasted kentish cobnuts, hay dressing and nasturtium
	Thomas Straker	*Casa Cruz*	Potato gnocchi with gorgonzola and spinach
	Jun Tanaka	*The Ninth*	Iberico pork pluma with herb vinaigrette and Piquillo peppers
	James and Chris Tanner	*Kentish Hare*	Kentish hare pork plate
	Robin Tarver	*Madison*	Roast wild halibut with smoked eel and leek fondue, and Avruga caviar
	Ben Ternent	*Opus at Cornwall Street*	Roasted monkfish tail with potato gnocchi, chanterelle's and shellfish sauce
	Stephen Terry	*The Hardwick*	Chargrilled pepper with mozzarella and pesto
	Phil Thompson	*Thompson St Albans*	Poached and roasted wood pigeon with confit leg pastilla, red cabbage and pear
	Eran Tibi	*Bala Baya*	Fish and fennel

Foodie fact #22
In an emergency coconut
water can be used as a
substitute for blood plasma.

James and Chris Tanner - *Kentish Hare*
Kentish Hare pork plate
Unlock these 250 recipes on the free CHARITABLE BOOKINGS lifestyle app.

RICK STEIN
The Seafood Restaurant

STEAMED MUSSELS with tomato and tarragon
SERVES 4 | PREPARATION TIME 15 MINUTES | COOKING TIME 10 MINUTES

For the Dish
30ml (*1.1fl oz*) extra virgin olive oil
2 cloves of garlic, finely chopped
1kg (*2.2lb*)mussels

30ml (*1.1fl oz*) dry white wine
30g (*1.1oz*) unsalted butter
60g (*2.2oz*) tomatoes, peeled, deseeded and finely chopped
5g (*0.18oz*) French tarragon, finely chopped
salt and pepper, to taste
For the Garnish
fresh bread or linguine

To prepare the dish, make sure the mussels are tightly closed. If they are fresh-farmed ones there is no need to wash them, but if they are showing any signs of grit or sand wash them in copious amounts of cold water.

Take a large saucepan, add the olive oil and garlic and soften over a medium heat for about a minute. Add the mussels, turn up the heat and add the white wine. Put a lid on the pan and cook for a few minutes until all the shells have opened, but only just. Stir the shells once or twice during the cooking to distribute them evenly. Remove and pour through a colander set over a bowl.

Keep the mussels warm while you transfer the liquor to a pan, heat until boiling, whisk in the butter then add the tomato and tarragon. Check the seasoning; it's always a good idea to leave seasoning to the end with shellfish as you never know how salty they are going to be, then add salt if necessary and freshly ground black pepper.

To serve, add the mussels back into the pan and plate with plenty of crusty bread or alternatively with a mound of al dente linguine pasta.

STEPHEN TERRY
The Hardwick

CHARGRILLED PEPPER with mozzarella and pesto
SERVES 4 | PREPARATION TIME 15 MINUTES | COOKING TIME 10 MINUTES

For the Vegetables and Mozzarella
2 large yellow or red peppers
8 large leaves radicchio lettuce
4 x 100g (*3.5oz*) balls buffalo mozzarella
1 shallot, peeled

For the Pickled Kohlrabi
vinegar, to cover
1 chilli, halved
1 small kohlrabi, peeled and diced

To Serve
4 tbsp good quality pesto
12 radishes, finely sliced
2 tbsp extra virgin olive oil
lemon juice and sea salt, to taste

To prepare the dish, chargrill the peppers, then peel them. Remove the seeds and cut the flesh into 4 equal pieces. Lightly chargrill the radicchio lettuce leaves. Slice each mozzarella ball into quarters. Finely slice the shallot and deep fry until crispy. You can put the peppers under the grill or use a blowtorch, both methods work equally well.

To make the pickled kohlrabi, bring the vinegar to the boil in a pan with the chilli, pour it over the kohlrabi and leave to pickle until the liquid has cooled.

To plate, layer the mozzarella and grilled pepper with pesto. Dress the radicchio and radish with olive oil and lemon juice. Season with salt. Finish by garnishing the radicchio with the diced kohlrabi and fried shallots and serve as pictured.

	Kevin Tickle	*The Forest Side*	Line-caught halibut with oyster dressing, caviar, charred lettuce and dittander
	Patrick Till	*Thackeray's*	Salt marsh hogget with cannon, shoulder suet pie, heritage carrots, spiced cous cous, caper and raisin purée
	Stephen Toman	*OX*	Halibut with curry, romanesco, bergamot and oyster leaf
	Matthew Tomkinson	*The Terrace at the Montagu Arms*	Spiced diver caught Scottish scallops with cauliflower purée, apple, coriander and cumin velouté
	Jeremy Trehout	*Plateau*	Roasted rack of lamb with aubergine confit, couscous and dukkah spice
	Marcello Tully	*Kinloch Lodge*	Duck breast and wilted spinach with orange, tomato and chilli dressing
	Stefano Turconi	*Franco's*	Porcini mushroom risotto
	Andrew Turner	*Alfred's*	Line-caught sea bass fillet with red pepper purée, young fennel and smoked olive oil
	Alex Tyndall	*Wheeler's restaurant in Threadneedles Hotel*	Ragu of vegetables and pulses with a smoked oyster dressing
	James Tyrrell	*L'Escargot*	Chilli crab on toast

Foodie fact #23
The ice lolly, or popsicle as it is known in the U.S.A., was invented by 11 year old Frank Epperson in 1905.

Stephen Toman – OX
Halibut with curry, romanesco, bergamot and oyster leaf
Unlock these 250 recipes on the free **CHARITABLE BOOKINGS** lifestyle app

MARCELLO TULLY

Kinloch Lodge

DUCK BREAST AND WILTED SPINACH with orange, tomato and chilli dressing

SERVES 2 | PREPARATION TIME 30 MINUTES | COOKING TIME 45 MINUTES

For the Duck
1 duck breast, with skin on
salt and pepper
For the Orange, Tomato and Chilli Dressing
20g (0.7oz) fresh ginger, finely chopped
2 cloves of garlic, finely chopped

10g (0.35oz) red chilli, finely chopped
10g (0.35oz) green chilli, finely chopped
2 oranges, juice and zest
2 tbsp cornflour, diluted with a little cold water
10g (0.35oz) caster sugar

1 pinch of salt
1 dash of Tabasco
50g (0.53oz) tomato concasse
For the Wilted Spinach
20ml (0.7fl oz) sunflower oil
200g (7oz) baby leaf spinach
salt and black pepper

To prepare the duck breast, remove any fatty sinews and score the skin. Heat a heavy-based frying pan, without any oil, and put the duck breast in, skin-side down. Fry until the skin renders and turns to a golden brown. Turn the breast over and place in a preheated oven at 180°C (355°F) for 2 minutes. Take out and turn over, then return to the oven for a further 1 minute. Allow the duck breast to rest for 3 minutes in a warm place, then carve into thin slices.

For the dressing, sweat the ginger, garlic and chillies for 2–3 minutes. Add the orange juice and zest, and bring to the boil. Whilst the liquid is boiling, add the cornflour and whisk in thoroughly. Add the caster sugar, salt and Tabasco, and mix. Remove from the stove. Add the tomato concassé, stir and serve.

To make the wilted spinach, heat the oil in a heavy based pan, add the spinach and turn with a large spoon. Remove from the pan as soon as the spinach starts to wilt, this should take approximately 30 seconds to 1 minute.

Serve the duck slices on a bed of wilted spinach and drizzle with the sauce.

STEFANO TURCONI

Franco's

PORCINI MUSHROOM RISOTTO

SERVES 4 | PREPARATION TIME 15 MINUTES | COOKING TIME 30 MINUTES

For the Risotto
80g (2.8oz) carnaroli rice
10g (0.35oz) dried porcini
mushrooms

30g (1.1oz) butter
30g (1.1oz) Parmesan
½ onion, finely chopped
½ glass of white wine

1l (35fl oz) vegetable stock
10 parsley leaves
1 pinch of salt

To make the risotto, soak the dried porcini mushrooms in cold water for 10 minutes. While the mushrooms soak, finely chop the onion. Lightly toast the rice in a pan for 3 minutes on a medium heat, with half the butter and the chopped onion. Add the white wine and stir together.

When the wine has evaporated, add the porcini mushrooms and slowly ladle in the vegetable stock, continue to do so for 15 minutes. Once the rice is cooked through, add the remaining butter along with the parsley and Parmesan and mix together.

Season with salt and leave to rest for 1 minute to allow the dish to thicken, then serve.

	Francisco D.R. Vilela	*La Poule au Pot*	Poule au pot
	Simon Wadham	*Rivington Greenwich*	Rivington Grill's Newlyn cod with crispy bacon, lovage and peas
	Steve Walker	*Sirocco at The Royal Yacht*	Fillet of Jersey beef with morels, asparagus and beef cheek
	Gareth Ward	*Ynyshir Hall*	Salt Welsh Wagyu rib - shiitake
	Marcus Wareing	*Marcus*	Herdwick lamb with beetroot and girolles
	Andy Waters	*Waters Restaurant*	Salmon in spicy coconut cream
	Emily Watkins	*The Kingham Plough*	Venison loin and black pudding with heritage beetroots and millet risotto
	Bryan Webb	*Tyddyn Llan*	Roast wild bass with laverbread butter sauce
	Paul Wedgewood	*Wedgewood The Restaurant*	Sesame roasted sea trout with braised pak choi, lobster and black bean nori roll and lobster mayonnaise
	Paul Welburn	*The Oxford Kitchen*	Beer and barley glazed pichana steak with celeriac, monks beard, salsa verde and smoked leeks

Foodie fact #24
Apples float because they consist of 25% air.

Matthew **Tomkinson** - *The Terrace at the Montagu Arms*
Spiced diver caught Scottish scallops with cauliflower purée, apple, coriander and cumin velouté
Unlock these 250 recipes on the free CHARITABLE BOOKINGS lifestyle app.

SIMON WADHAM

Rivington Greenwich

RIVINGTON GRILL'S NEWLYN COD with crispy bacon, lovage and peas

SERVES 4 | PREPARATION TIME 15 MINUTES | COOKING TIME 40 MINUTES

For the Cod
4 x 180g (6.3oz) cod fillets,
skin on
200g (7oz) fresh peas, podded
extra virgin olive oil, for cooking
1 shallot, finely diced

120g (4.2oz) streaky bacon or
pancetta, cut into 1cm strips
50ml (1.8fl oz) white wine
1 head little gem lettuce, finely
shredded
10 lovage leaves, roughly

chopped
70g (2.5oz) unsalted butter,
chilled and diced
salt and freshly ground black
pepper
½ lemon, juiced

To prepare the dish, bring a saucepan of water to the boil, add the peas and cook until tender. Drain and keep to one side. Heat the olive oil in a heavy-bottomed saucepan. Add the shallot and bacon and cook for 2 minutes, allowing them to colour lightly. Add the wine, reduce by a third and add the peas, lettuce, lovage and butter. Stir well, season and cook for a further 2 minutes. Take off the heat and keep warm.

To cook the cod, heat a non stick frying pan, brush the cod with oil, place in a pan flesh side down and cook for 7 minutes. Turn over and cook for a further 4 minutes, or until the cod is just cooked through.

Place on a plate and spoon some of the peas, lettuce and lovage mixture over and around the fish. Spritz with lemon juice and serve immediately.

ANDY WATERS
Waters Restaurant

SALMON IN SPICY COCONUT CREAM
SERVES 4 | PREPARATION TIME 15 MINUTES | COOKING TIME 30 MINUTES

For the Salmon
4 salmon fillets
2 tsp peanut oil
2 cloves of garlic, crushed
5g (0.18oz) fresh ginger, grated
20g (0.7oz) turmeric, fresh,
finely grated

2 small red chillies, thinly sliced
355ml (12.5fl oz) fish stock
400ml (14fl oz) coconut cream
20g fresh lemongrass
2 tbsp fish sauce
2 green onions, thinly sliced
1 pak choi, 8 small leaves

For the Garnish
4 cherry tomatoes
1 red chilli, sliced
edible flowers
4 dried bay leaves
1 tbsp sesame seeds

To begin, place a frying pan over a high heat and add the peanut oil. Once hot, stir-fry the garlic, ginger, turmeric and chilli until fragrant, then add the stock, coconut cream and lemongrass and bring to the boil.

Once boiling, add the salmon fillets so they are immersed in the sauce and flat. Lower the heat, cover the pan and simmer for approximately 8 minutes, or until the fish is just cooked through.

Using a slotted spoon, carefully remove the fillets from the sauce and place in a serving bowl, covering to keep warm. Remove the lemongrass from the sauce and discard. Bring the sauce back to the boil and cook for 5 minutes to reduce and thicken slightly.

Remove the sauce from the heat and stir in the fish sauce, sliced green onions and pak choi.

Place the salmon fillets into bowls and pour the sauce on top. Decorate with dried bay leaves, edible flowers, sliced red chilli and cherry tomatoes. Sprinkle with sesame seeds and serve immediately with steamed rice.

	Shaun Whatling	*The Berkeley Hotel*	Pan seared Angus beef medallion with sautéed ceps , curly kale, roscoff onions and bone marrow
	John Williams	*The Ritz*	Roast grouse with celeriac, salted grapes and walnuts
	Alyn Williams	*Alyn Williams at The Westbury*	Roasted monkfish with fennel compote, grapefruit, coconut, cashews and roche carré
	Martin Wishart	*Restaurant Martin Wishart*	Langoustine ravioli with braised orange endive and langoustine jus
	Mike Womersley	*The Three Lions*	Galette of smoked haddock
	Kim Woodward	*Skylon*	Roasted monkfish with textures of fennelandlobster bisque
	Mark Woolgar	*Ampersand Hotel*	Stone bass ceviche
	Victor Yu	*Yu Alderley Edge*	Marinated black cod with champagne and miso
	Chris Zachwieja	*Boisdale of Belgravia*	Ravioli of cornish monkfish with hebridean langoustine, shellfish bisque, confit tomatoes and wild sea greens
	Sasha Ziverts	*The Wright Brothers Soho*	Black pepper crab

Foodie fact #25
Most Wasabi eaten is in fact just
dyed horseradish.

Marcus **Wareing** - *Marcus*
Herdwick lamb with beetroot and girolles
Unlock these 250 recipes on the free CHARITABLE BOOKINGS lifestyle app.

VICTOR YU

Yu Alderley Edge

MARINATED BLACK COD with Champagne and miso

SERVES 2 | PREPARATION TIME 6 HOURS | COOKING TIME 15 MINUTES

For the Marinade
25ml *(0.9fl oz)* mirin
65ml *(2.3fl oz)* Shaoshing rice wine
25g *(0.9oz)* caster sugar
25ml *(0.9fl oz)* Champagne

75g *(2.6oz)* miso paste
For the Garnish
selection of herbs and edible flowers
1 tbsp olive oil

For the Cod
2 x 125g *(4.4oz)* black cod fillets

For the marinade, pour the mirin, Shaoshing rice wine and caster sugar into a saucepan and bring to the boil. Once the sugar has dissolved and the liquid is at a rolling boil, remove from the heat and allow to cool for a minute. Add the Champagne and miso paste into the pan and whisk until smooth. Set aside until cooled down completely.

To prepare the cod, check the fish over to make sure all the skin and bones have been removed. Place into a sealable sandwich bag and pour in the cooled mixture. Extract as much air from the bag as possible, seal and give the fish a gentle rub so that it is well covered. Leave to marinate in the fridge for a minimum of 6 hours.

To cook the cod, preheat a fan oven to 220°C *(430°F)*, and line a shallow baking tray with parchment paper. Remove the fish from the bag and wipe away the majority of the marinade. Place the fish onto the prepared baking tray and bake in the oven for 12 minutes.

To serve, place the herbs in a small bowl and drizzle with the olive oil. Carefully place a portion of fish in the centre of a small warmed serving bowl and arrange a salad next to the fish. Serve immediately.

SASHA ZIVERTS
The Wright Brothers Soho

BLACK PEPPER CRAB

SERVES 2 | PREPARATION TIME 30 MINUTES | COOKING TIME 30 MINUTES

For the Crab
1 x 800g–1kg (*1.8lb-2.2lb*) whole, live cock crab
1 tbsp vegetable oil

For the Sauce
250g (*8.8oz*) salted butter
200g (*7oz*) shallots, finely chopped
50g (*1.8oz*) garlic, finely chopped
50g (*1.8oz*) ginger, finely chopped
100ml (*3.5fl oz*) Japanese soy sauce

80ml (*2.8fl oz*) mirin
30g (*1.1oz*) black pepper, freshly cracked
sugar, to taste

For the Garnish
almond slivers, toasted
curry leaves, deep fried
natural yoghurt

To prepare the crab, first despatch it humanely. Next, turn upside down and cut in half, removing the legs and dead man's fingers. Cut the crab into segments, cracking the larger pieces with the back of your knife and set aside.

To make the sauce, melt half the butter in a pan and add in the shallots, garlic and ginger. Cook on a low heat. When soft, add the soy sauce and mirin. When the mixture is reduced by half, add the black pepper and the rest of the butter. Season with a little sugar and set aside.

Heat a saucepan and add the vegetable oil. When smoking, add the crab pieces and a small amount of sauce to start the cooking process. Once evaporated, stir the crab well and add the rest of the sauce. Cook for 8–10 minutes.

To serve, arrange the plate as pictured and spoon over the remaining sauce. Garnish with toasted almonds, deep fried curry leaves and fresh natural yoghurt.

Recipe Index

MEAT

POULTRY

DUCK

Crispy duck salad	*36*
Roast Gressingham duck with caramelised carrot pureé, roast carrots and fig jus	*84*
Duck breast and wilted spinach with orange, tomato and chilli dressing	*156*

GAME

GROUSE

Wiltons' roast grouse	*120*

PHEASANT

Roast pheasant and winter vegetables	*48*

RABBIT

Miso glazed rabbit with cauliflower pureé and pie crust	*62*

VENISON

Loin of venison with poached pear and blue cheese gratin	*74*

FISH

BREAM

Black bream ceviche	*54*

COD

Cornish cod à la Grenobloise	*50*
Tandoori spiced cod with leek, spring onions and capers	*102*
Rivington Grill's Newlyn cod with crispy bacon, lovage and peas	*162*
Marinated black cod with Champagne and miso	*168*

HADDOCK

Cullen skink	*78*

HAKE

Hake with romesco crust	*104*

HALIBUT

Halibut steak with new season peas à la française	*38*

RED MULLET

Baked red mullet with Taggiasche olives and tomato	*144*

SABLEFISH

Caramelised sablefish with vegetable spaghetti	*138*

SALMON

Salmon in spicy coconut cream	*164*

SEA BASS

Sea bass with miso glaze, baby spinach, fennel, pomodori secchi	72
Masala sea bass	108
Stone bass ceviche	134

SKATE

Skate wing a la Grenobloise with seaweed	122

TURBOT

Steamed Cornish turbot with line-caught squid and dashi	96

SHELLFISH

CRAB

Black pepper crab	170

MUSSELS

Mussels steamed with lemongrass, basil chilli and coconut juice	68
Steamed mussels with tomato and tarragon	150

OYSTERS

Crispy Porthilly oysters	26
Crisp Loch Creran oysters with sauce gribiche	92

PRAWNS

Saffron prawns with fennel	140

SCALLOPS

Roast scallops with polenta and squid ink sauce	30
White onion risotto with white chocolate, scallops and white truffle	56

VEGETARIAN

VEGETARIAN

Samba salad	60
Stracciatella ricotta tortelli	126
BBQ onion with potato gnocchi, avocado, brazil nuts and burnt onion crème fraîche	146
Chargrilled pepper with mozzarella and pesto	152
Porcini mushroom risotto	158

OTHER

NON-VEGETARIAN CHEESE DISHES

Roasted cauliflower with lemon curry infused oil and aged Parmesan	90

Acknowledgements

I would like to thank the following for their invaluable assistance and encouragement in taking this concept and turning it into this beautiful book collection.

We gratefully acknowledge the chefs, restaurants and their teams, agents and PRs in supplying the recipes and images of the dishes and in helping us to support so many good causes.

Thanks to our many supporters who have embraced CHARITABLE **BOOKINGS** including Free Holdings, Gravity Integrated Solutions, Pearl DME, Palladium PR, Relish Publications, Part & Company, Seasoned by Chefs, Camille Percheron, Alexandra Preda-Ralev, Violeta Martinez, Alon Shulman, Charlotte Tyson, Deborah Mack, Francesca Di Belmonte, Kasia Szelagowska, Laragh Chambers, Lucy Self, Michael Korel, Richa Verma, Sophie Elbrick, Blessing Zidyarukwa, Alina Pacurar, Will Rockall, Alp Ozen, Helen Mason-Belshaw, Veronique Cabrol, Mantus Siurkus, Ken Fung, Sultan Malik, Marzena Drewniak, Lina Benfarhat, Susanna Jennens, Duncan Peters, Valerie McLeod and Andy Richardson.

With thanks to the many photographers who have supported the chefs and restaurants by providing them with images including: David Griffen, Palida Boonyarungsrit, John Blackwell, John Carey, Thomas Alexander, Jean Cazals, Lara Messer, Great British Chefs, Jacqui Small, Tim Green, Jo Woodhouse, Paul Johnston, photo of Paul Ainsworth by David Williams, Marcus Bean's recipe photo ©Watkins Media Ltd. Every effort has been made to acknowledge all the photographers. If you have provided a photo and not been credited, please let us know so we can add you to the next edition.

MORE BOOKS IN THE COLLECTION AVAILABLE AT

charitable**bookings**.com/**recipe-books**

ISBN: 978-0-9957116-1-7

FH PUBLISHING
Published in London by FH Publishing
fhpublishing.com

"The perfect gift for all foodies..."